Kind

Social Studies

Daily Practice Workbook

20 weeks of fun activities

History • **Civics and Government** • **Geography** • **Economics**

ArgoPrep is one of the leading providers of supplemental educational products and services. We offer affordable and effective test prep solutions to educators, parents and students. Learning should be fun and easy! To access more resources visit us at www.argoprep.com.

Our goal is to make your life easier, so let us know how we can help you by e-mailing us at: info@argoprep.com.

- ArgoPrep is a recipient of the prestigious **Mom's Choice Award**.
- ArgoPrep also received the 2019 **Seal of Approval** from Homeschool.com for our award-winning workbooks.
- ArgoPrep was awarded the 2019 **National Parenting Products Award**, **Gold Medal Parent's Choice Award** and **the Tillywig Brain Child Award.**

ISBN: 9781951048686

Published by Argo Brothers.

SOCIAL STUDIES

Social Studies Daily Practice Workbook by ArgoPrep allows students to build foundational skills and review concepts. Our workbooks explore social studies topics in depth with ArgoPrep's 5 E's to build social studies mastery.

OTHER BOOKS BY ARGOPREP

Here are some other test prep workbooks by ArgoPrep you may be interested in. All of our workbooks come equipped with detailed video explanations to make your learning experience a breeze! Visit us at www.argoprep.com

COMMON CORE MATH SERIES

COMMON CORE ELA SERIES

INTRODUCING MATH!

Introducing Math! by ArgoPrep is an award-winning series created by certified teachers to provide students with high-quality practice problems. Our workbooks include topic overviews with instruction, practice questions, answer explanations along with digital access to video explanations. Practice in confidence - with ArgoPrep!

SCIENCE SERIES

Science Daily Practice Workbook by ArgoPrep is an award-winning series created by certified science teachers to help build mastery of foundational science skills. Our workbooks explore science topics in depth with ArgoPrep's 5 E'S to build science mastery.

KIDS SUMMER ACADEMY SERIES

ArgoPrep's Kids Summer Academy series helps prevent summer learning loss and gets students ready for their new school year by reinforcing core foundations in math, english and science. Our workbooks also introduce new concepts so students can get a head start and be on top of their game for the new school year!

WATER FIRE

GREEN
POISON

FIRESTORM
WARRIOR

RAPID NINJA

CAPTAIN
ARGO

THUNDER
WARRIOR

DANCE HERO

ADRASTOS THE
SUPER WARRIOR

CAPTAIN
BRAVERY

Introduction

Welcome to our kindergarten social studies workbook!

This workbook has been specifically designed to help students build mastery of foundational social studies skills that are taught in kindergarten. Included are 20 weeks of comprehensive instruction covering the four branches of social studies: History, Civics and Government, Geography, and Economics.

This workbook dedicates five weeks of instruction to each of the four branches of social studies, focusing on different standards within each week of instruction.

Within the branch of History, students will make connections between their own environment and the past. In Civics and Government, they will learn more about community helpers and what it means to be a citizen. Students will dive into the physical and geographical characteristics of their community in Geography. Finally, in the Economics section, they will have the opportunity to learn about different jobs and basic economic needs.

At the conclusion of the 20 weeks of instruction, students should have a solid grasp of the concepts required by the National Council for Social Studies for kindergarten.

Table of Contents

How to Use the Book

All 20 weeks of daily activity pages in this book follow the same weekly structure. The four sections should read: History, Civics and Government, Geography, Economics. The activities in each of the sections align to the concepts required by the National Council for the Social Studies. While the sections can be completed in any order, it is important to complete each week within the section in chronological order since the skills often build upon each other.

Each week focuses on one specific topic within the section. More information about the weekly structure can be found in the Weekly Planner section.

Weekly Planner

Day	Activity	Description
1	Engaging with the Topic	Read a short text on the topic and answer multiple choice questions.
2	Exploring the Topic	Interact with the topic on a deeper level by diving further into the concept and its sub-concepts.
3	Explaining the Topic	Make sense of the topic by explaining and beginning to draw conclusions about the topic.
4	Experiencing the Topic	Investigate the topic by connecting it to real-life experiences.
5	Elaborating on the Topic	Reflect on the topic and use all information learned to draw conclusions and evaluate results.

List of Topics

Unit	Week	Topic
History	1	Children and Families: Past and Present
History	2	Famous People in History
History	3	Famous Events in History
History	4	Sequencing Events
History	5	Calendars
Civics and Government	6	Community Helpers
Civics and Government	7	The President of the United States
Civics and Government	8	The American Flag
Civics and Government	9	The Importance of Rules
Civics and Government	10	Being a Good Citizen
Geography	11	Maps and Globes
Geography	12	Addresses
Geography	13	Weather
Geography	14	Human Systems
Geography	15	Improving Our Environment
Economics	16	Wants and Needs
Economics	17	Jobs - Part 1
Economics	18	Jobs - Part 2
Economics	19	Choosing a Job
Economics	20	Working at Home

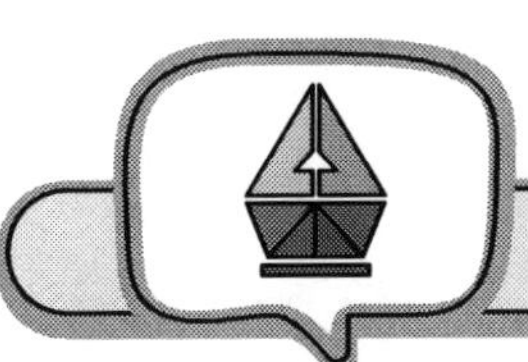

How to access video explanations?

Go to **argoprep.com/socialK**
OR scan the QR Code:

WEEK 1

History

Children and Families: Past and Present

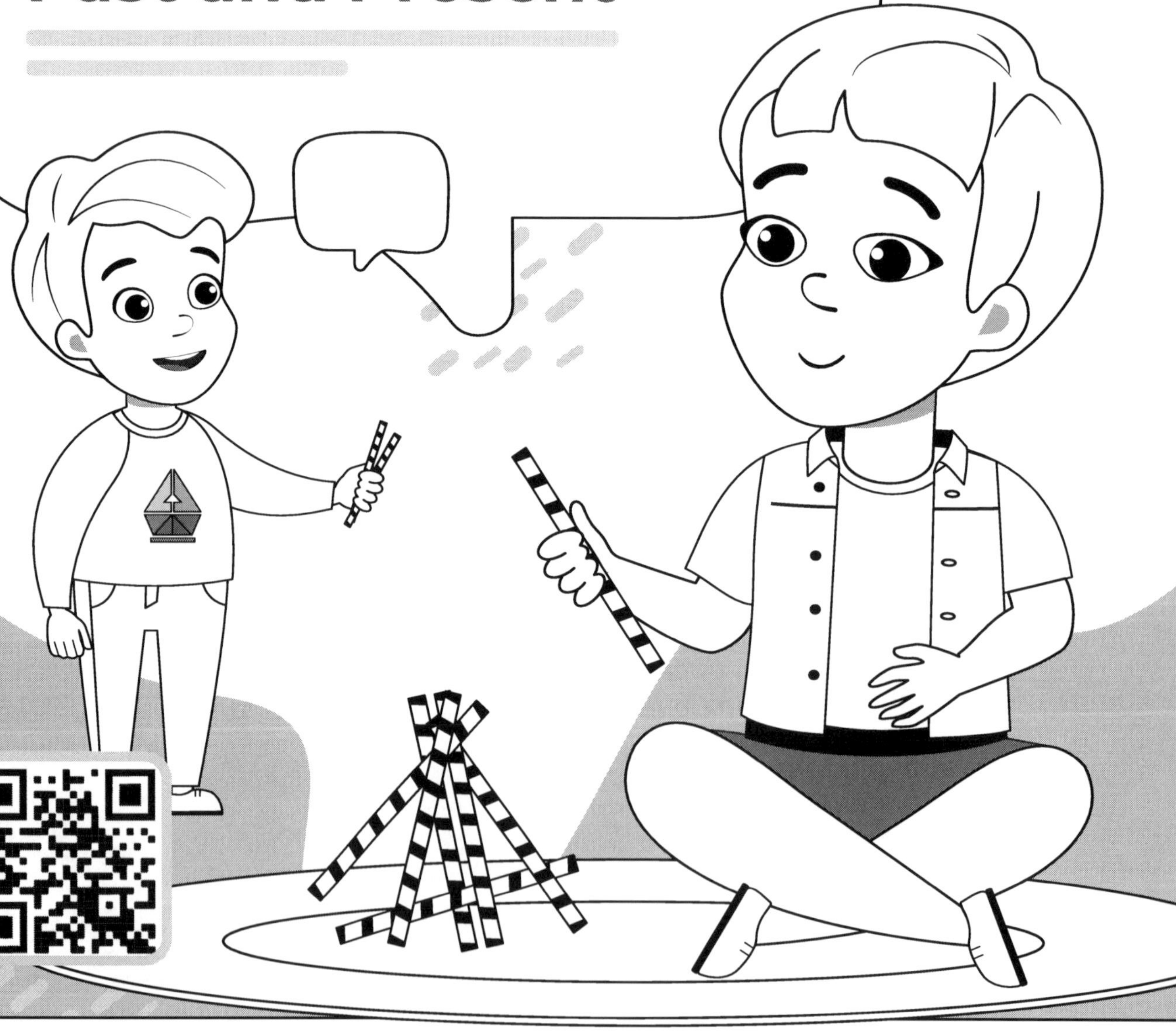

Compare children and families of today with those of the past.

Directions: Read the text below. Then answer the questions that follow.

Children and Families of the Past

A long time ago, many things were different from how they are now. Houses and clothing looked different. Children played with different toys and games. They did not have many of the toys you may have now like video games and tablets. People ate different things and had different modes of transportation than what we have today. Do you think you would have enjoyed living in the past?

1. Children and families in the past were different from how they are now.

   A. True

   B. False

2. What types of things were different long ago?

   A. Toys and games

   B. Houses

   C. Clothing

   D. All of the above

3. A long time ago, children played with tablets and video games.

   A. True

   B. False

Yesterday you learned that children and families were different in the past. Today you will explore what parts of life were different in the past.

Directions: Read the words below. Decide whether or not they were different in the past from how they are now.

Clothing	Houses	Food
Toys and Games	Tools	Transportation

Directions: Write each word in the correct column below.

Same	Different

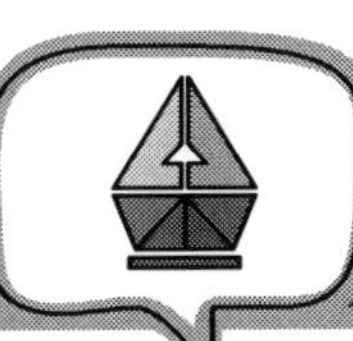

Yesterday you learned that many things were different in the past. Today you will explain how they were different.

Directions: Draw pictures below to show what each thing might have looked like in the past.

Clothing	
Toys and Games	
Houses	

You have spent several days learning, exploring, and explaining how life was different in the past. Today you will play a game that children enjoyed playing in the past.

The Game:

Pick Up Sticks

Materials:

1. 10-20 straws or wooden skewers

To Play:

1. Put the straws or skewers in a pile in the middle of the players.
2. Taking turns, each person should remove one straw or skewer from the pile without moving any of the other straws or skewers.
3. Players are out if they move straws or skewers other than the one they are removing.

Follow-Up Questions:

1. What might children have used instead of straws or wooden skewers to play this game in the past?

2. Who played the game with you?

3. Who won the game?

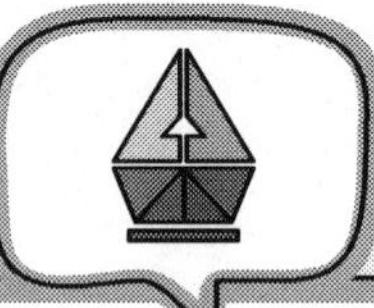

Yesterday you played a game that was popular with children in the past. Today you will reflect on what life might have been like for children in the past.

Directions: Read and answer each question below.

1. Draw a picture of something you would like about living in the past.

2. Draw a picture of something you like about living now.

3. Would you rather live in:

A. The past

B. The present (right now)

WEEK 2

History

Famous People in History

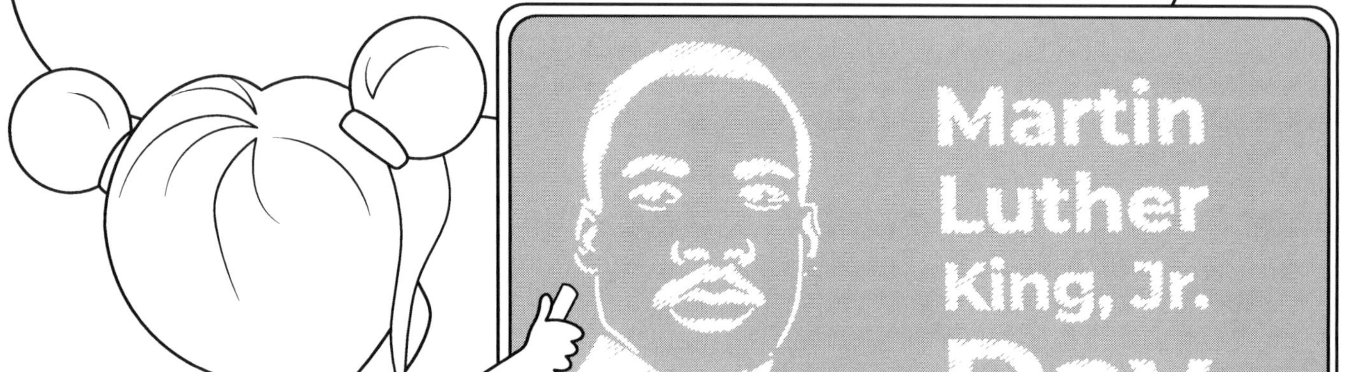

Martin Luther King, Jr. Day

Identify ways in which famous people from history are celebrated.

Directions: Read the text below. Then answer the questions that follow.

Dr. Martin Luther King, Jr.

Throughout history, many people have played an important role in making our country better. One of these people is Dr. Martin Luther King, Jr. He was a civil rights leader who fought for equal rights for African Americans and believed in peace. We now celebrate Martin Luther King, Jr. on the third Monday of January each year. Dr. Martin Luther King, Jr. Day is a way Americans can recognize and celebrate the great things he did for civil rights in our country.

1. Dr. Martin Luther King, Jr. was an important person in our country's history.

A. True
B. False

2. Dr. Martin Luther King, Jr. was a:

A. Doctor
B. Civil Rights leader
C. Police Officer
D. Teacher

3. Why do we celebrate Dr. Martin Luther King, Jr. each year?

A. It's his birthday.
B. He was a President.
C. He was an important leader and did great things for our country.
D. He was a famous teacher.

Yesterday you learned that Dr. Martin Luther King, Jr. was an important person in history. Today you will explore the good things he did for our country.

Directions: Read the text below.

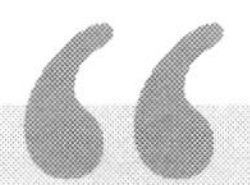

Dr. Martin Luther King, Jr. worked hard for equal rights for African Americans. During his lifetime, people with different colors of skin did not have the same rights as white people. Dr. Martin Luther King, Jr. did not think that was fair. He thought everyone should be treated equally and have equal rights like being able to vote. Some people were fighting for equal rights by causing destruction or hurting others. Dr. Martin Luther King, Jr. believed in peace and being kind to others. He led people to do the same by giving speeches, protesting peacefully, and showing his disagreement with things he thought were unfair.

Directions: Read each word in the word bank. Decide whether it was one of Dr. Martin Luther King, Jr.'s beliefs or actions. Write each word in the correct column below.

Equal Rights
Peace and Kindness
Gave Speeches
Inspired Others
Led Protests
Ability to Vote

Beliefs	Actions

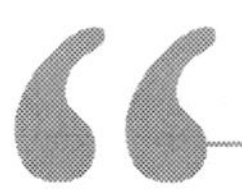

Yesterday you learned about the important things Dr. Martin Luther King, Jr. did for our country. Today you will explain why these things were important.

Directions: Write a sentence below to explain why you think Dr. Martin Luther King, Jr. was an important person. Draw a picture to go with your sentence.

Dr. Martin Luther King, Jr. was an important person because

You have spent several days learning, exploring, and explaining how Dr. Martin Luther King, Jr. was important. Today you will list different ways you could celebrate his life on Martin Luther King, Jr. Day in January.

I could celebrate Dr. Martin Luther King, Jr.'s life by:

1. ....

....

....

2. ....

....

....

3. ....

....

....

4. ....

....

....

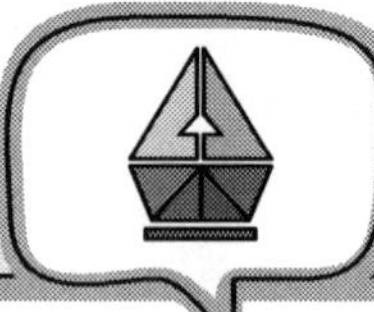

Yesterday you thought of ways you could celebrate Dr. Martin Luther King, Jr.'s life. Today you will reflect on why it is important to celebrate famous people from history.

Directions: Read and answer each question below.

1. Why do you think it's important to celebrate important people from our country's history?

2. Who are some other important people in our country's history we should celebrate?

3. Draw a picture of how you might celebrate a famous person from history.

WEEK 3

History

Famous Events in History

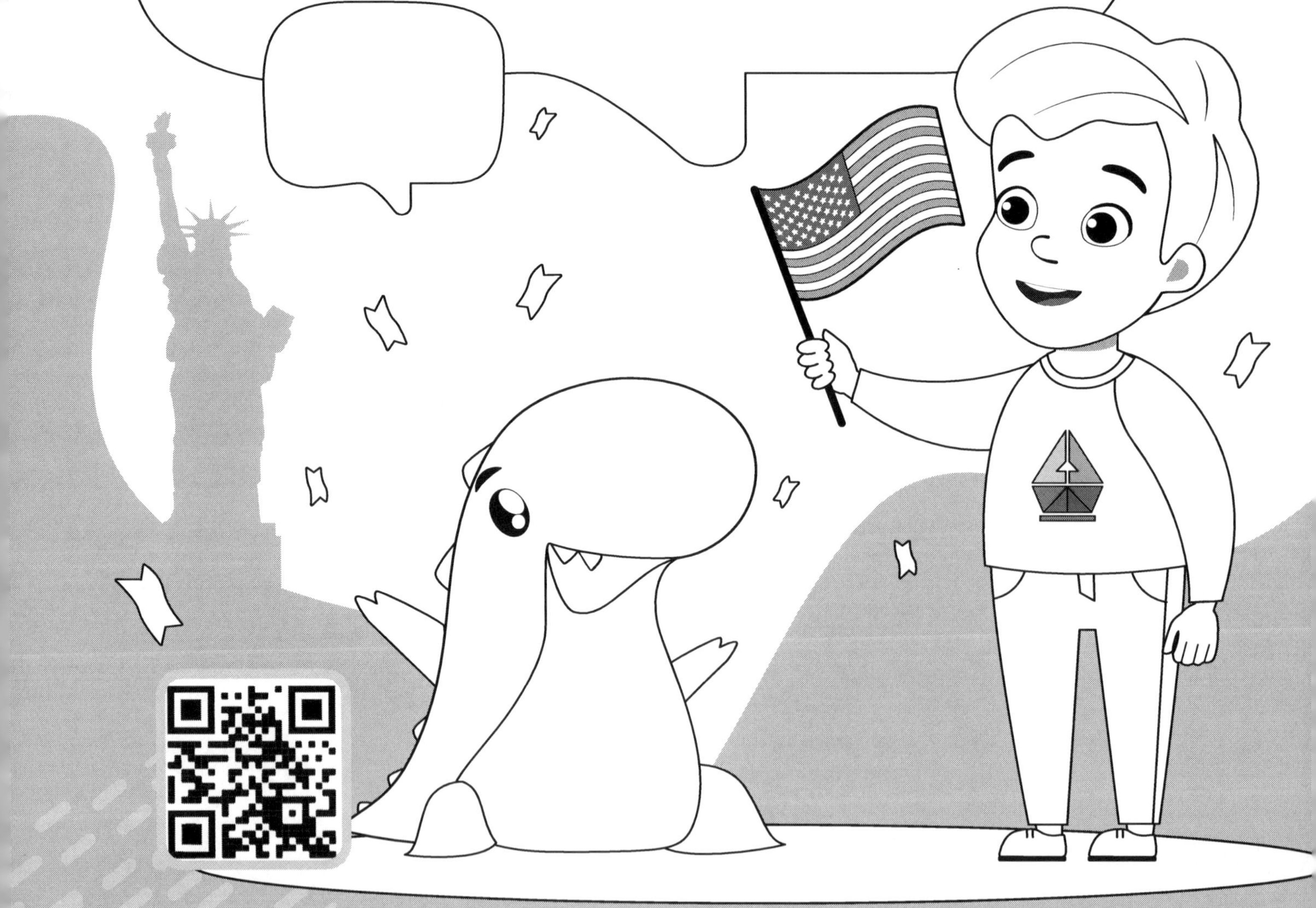

Identify ways in which important events are commemorated and celebrated.

Directions: Read the text below. Then answer the questions that follow.

Independence Day

Over time, many events have happened that are important to our country's history. One of these events was the day our country declared independence from Great Britain by approving the **Declaration of Independence,** a very important document in our nation's history. This day is often referred to as America's birthday or Independence Day. We celebrate Independence Day on the 4th of July each year. This is a day Americans can recognize and celebrate when our country became a free country.

1. Independence Day is not really an important event in our country's history.

A. True

B. False

2. Independence Day is the day our country:

A. Was ruled by Great Britain

B. Became free

C. Approved the Declaration of Independence

D. Both B and C

3. The Declaration of Independence was:

A. An important document

B. The document that made America free

C. Approved on July 4

D. All of the above

Yesterday you learned that Independence Day was an important event in history. Today you will explore the ways we celebrate it.

Directions: Read the text below.

The United States of America became a country on July 4, 1776. This is the day the Declaration of Independence was signed by many important people. We now celebrate our country's birthday every year on the 4th of July. Many people celebrate this day by getting together with friends and family for picnics, parades, baseball games, and fireworks. The 4th of July is a fun day to celebrate!

Directions: Read each word in the word bank. Decide whether or not it is a way people usually celebrate Independence Day. Write each word in the correct column below.

Fireworks
Trick or Treating
Parade
Egg Hunt
Picnic
Decorating a Tree

Yes	No

Week 3 — Famous Events in History

Day 3 — EXPLAINING THE TOPIC

Yesterday you learned about the ways people celebrate Independence Day. Today you will explain why this day is important.

Directions: Write a sentence below to explain why you think Independence Day is an important event. Draw a picture to go with your sentence.

Independence Day is an important event because

You have spent several days learning, exploring, and explaining how Independence Day is important. Today you will list different ways your family celebrates Independence Day.

I celebrate Independence Day by:

1. ....

2. ....

3. ....

4. ....

Yesterday you listed ways you celebrate Independence Day with your family. Today you will reflect on why it is important to celebrate famous events from history.

Directions: Read and answer each question below.

1. Why do you think it's important to celebrate famous events from our country's history?

2. What are some other important events in our country's history that should be celebrated?

3. Draw a picture of how you might celebrate a famous event in history.

WEEK 4

History

Sequencing Events

Place events in a sequence.

ARGOPREP

Directions: Read the text below. Then answer the questions that follow.

What is Sequencing?

To **sequence** means to put things in a certain order. Think about how you count from 1-10. Numbers have a specific order. We always count 1, 2, 3, 4, 5, 6, 7, 8, 9, 10. Now think about the alphabet. Letters are just like numbers. The letters of the alphabet are in a specific order. Events in history can also be sequenced, or put in order, by the date on which they happened.

1. To sequence means to:

A. Say numbers or letters
B. Put things in order
C. Talk about things that happened a long time ago

2. Things can be sequenced by:

A. Date
B. Time
C. Number
D. All of the above

3. What types of things can be sequenced?

A. Numbers
B. Letters
C. Dates
D. All of the above

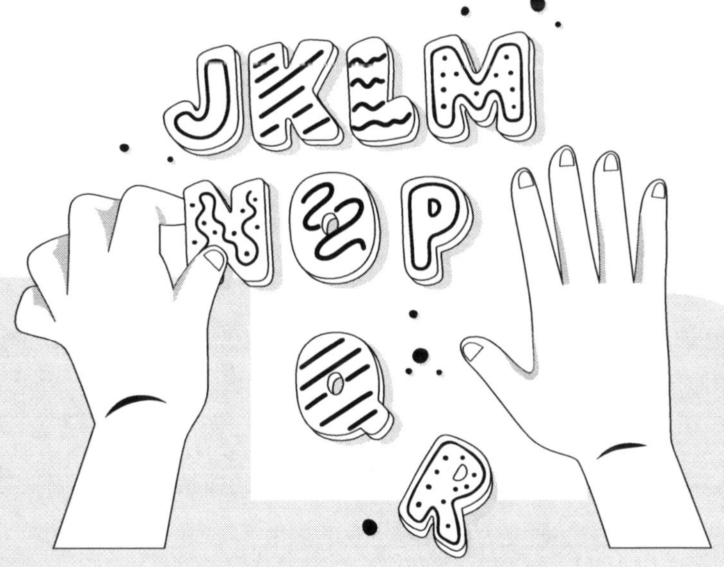

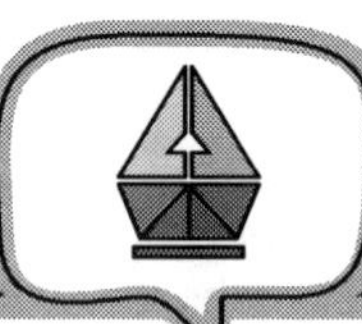

Sequencing Events

EXPLORING THE TOPIC

Yesterday you learned that to sequence means to put things in order. Today you will practice putting information in order.

Directions: Put each set of data, or information, in order.

1. Sequence the numbers.

5	**2**	**1**	**3**	**4**

2. Sequence the letters.

E	**A**	**D**	**B**	**C**

3. Sequence the times.

2:00	3:00	5:00	1:00	4:00

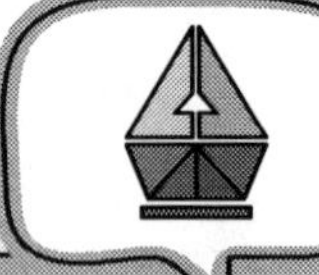

Sequencing Events

EXPLAINING THE TOPIC

Yesterday you practiced sequencing different sets of information. Today you will explain why sequencing is important.

Directions: Write a sentence below to explain why you think sequencing information is important. Give an example or draw a picture to go with your sentence.

Sequencing is important because:

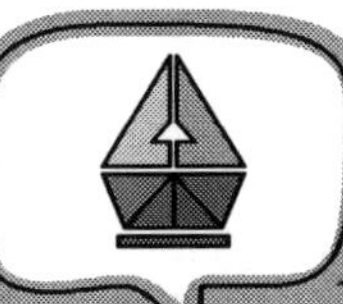

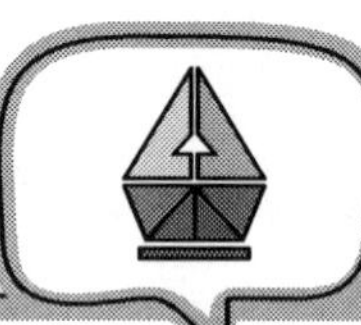

Sequencing Events

EXPERIENCING THE TOPIC

You have spent several days learning about, exploring, and explaining how sequencing is important. Today, you will create a timeline of your school day. First, you need to list the different parts of your school day and what time they happen.

1. List the different parts of your school day and what time they each happen on the table below.

Event	Time

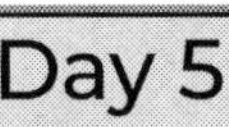

Yesterday you listed the different parts of your school day and what time each one happens. Today you will use the information from the table you made yesterday to create a timeline of your day.

Directions: Put each part of your school day in order based on the time it happens. You can create your timeline below or on a separate piece of paper.

WEEK 5

History

Calendars

Explain that calendars are used to represent the days of the week and the months of the year.

Directions: Read the text below. Then answer the questions that follow.

What is a Calendar?

A calendar is a chart that is used to represent the days of the week and the months of the year. Holidays and other special days are also usually marked on a calendar. A calendar is a very useful tool. They help people to keep track of when things are happening.

1. A calendar is:

A. A holiday or other special day
B. A tool that shows the days of the week and months of the year
C. A schedule

2. What things are usually found on a calendar?

A. Days of the week
B. Months of the year
C. Holidays
D. All of the above

3. Calendars are very useful to people.

A. True
B. False

Yesterday you learned that a calendar is a tool to help people keep track of days and months. Today you will explore the information found on a calendar.

Directions: Use a calendar to help you find and sequence the following information.

1. List the days of the week in order on the table below.

2. List the months of the year in order on the table below.

SUMMER

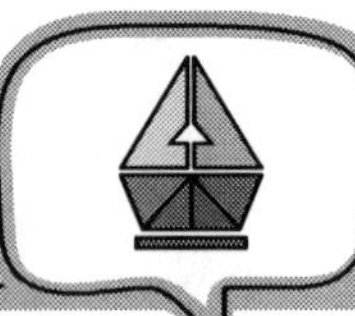

Week 5 Calendars

Day 3 EXPLAINING THE TOPIC

Yesterday you practiced sequencing different sets of information found on a calendar. Today you will explain what other information can be found on a calendar.

Directions: Use a calendar to help you answer each question below.

1. Find 5 holidays on the calendar. List them below.

2. Find 5 other things that are marked on the calendar that are NOT holidays. List them below.

3. If you were making a calendar of your own, what other special days would you want to include?

....

....

....

....

....

....

....

You have spent several days learning, exploring, and explaining how calendars work. Today you will create a calendar of your own. First, you need to list the holidays, special events, and other special days you want to include, as well as when they happen.

1. List the different days you want to include on your calendar on the table below. Be sure to include when each day happens during the year.

Holiday/Event/Special Day	Date

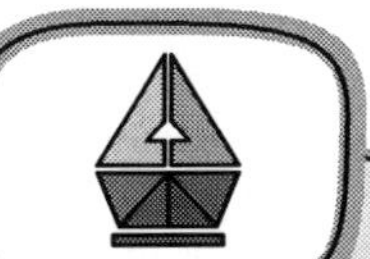

Week 5 — Calendars

Day 5 — ELABORATING ON THE TOPIC

Yesterday you listed the special days and events you want to include on your calendar. Today you will use the information from the table you made yesterday to create a calendar of your own.

Directions: Create your own calendar. It can be for one week, one month, or one year. Be sure to include the special days and events you listed yesterday. You can create your calendar below or on a separate piece of paper.

WEEK 6

Civics and Government

Community Helpers

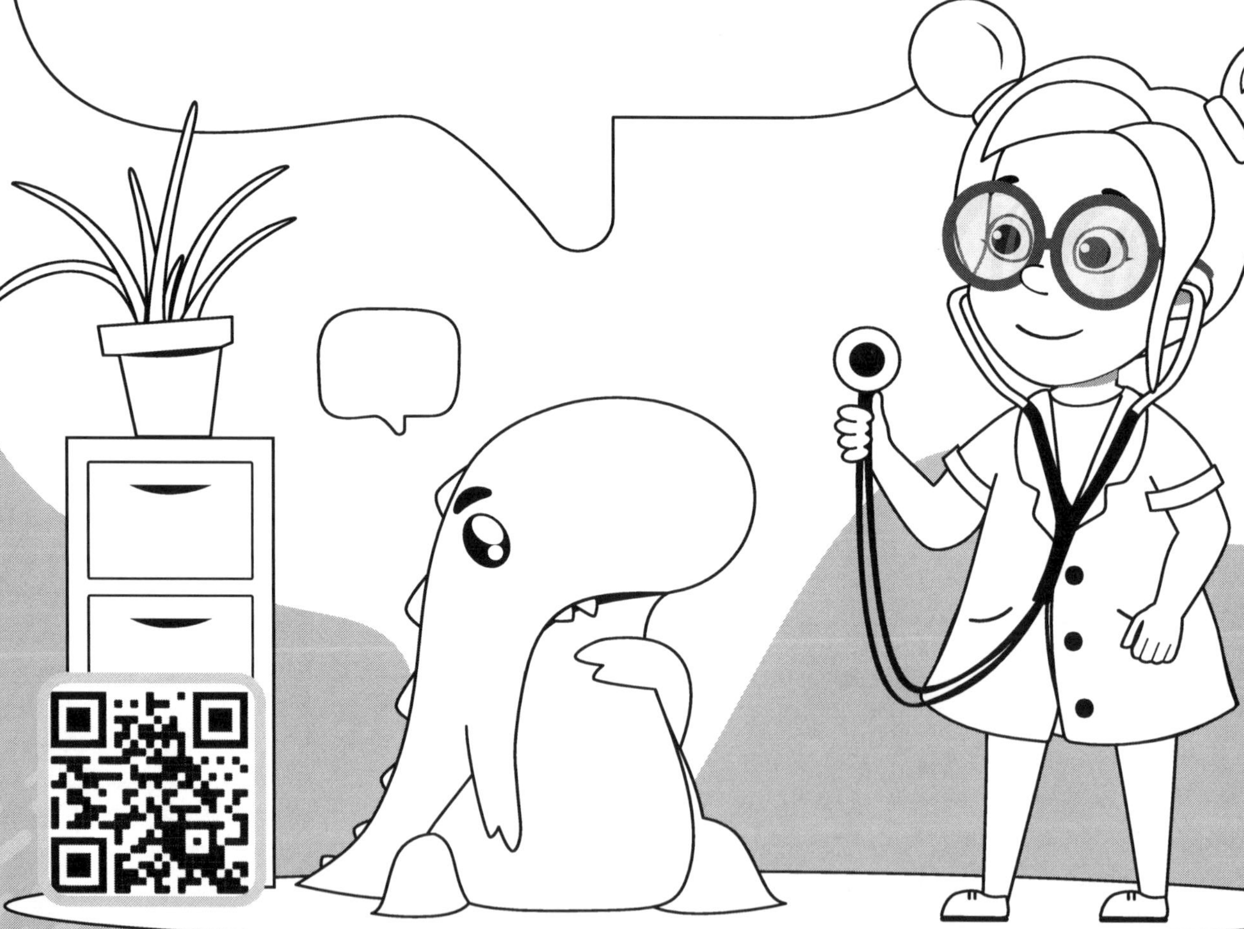

Give examples of people who are community helpers and describe how they help us.

Directions: Read the text below. Then answer the questions that follow.

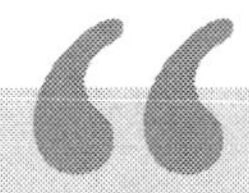

Community Helpers

Community helpers are people who are leaders of groups such as schools, neighborhoods, or cities. Their job is to help and protect the people in that community. A police officer is an example of a community helper. Their job is to keep people safe. Other examples of community helpers include: teachers, nurses, firefighters, and park rangers.

1. A community helper is:

A. A person who has a job
B. A person who teaches others
C. A person who helps others and keeps them safe

2. Which of the following are examples of a community?

A. A school
B. A neighborhood
C. A city
D. All of the above

3. Which of the following is NOT an example of a community helper?

A. Doctor
B. Mechanic
C. Actress
D. Teacher

Yesterday you learned that a community helper is a person who helps others and keeps them safe. Today you will explore what different community helpers do.

Directions: Read each description below. Choose the community helper you think does each job and write it on the line.

1. This community helper works in a building with many books. Their job is to help people find books they would like to read. Who is it?

2. This community helper loves animals and takes care of them when they are sick. Who is it?

3. This community helper drives a big truck and keeps people safe by putting out fires in houses and other buildings. Who is it?

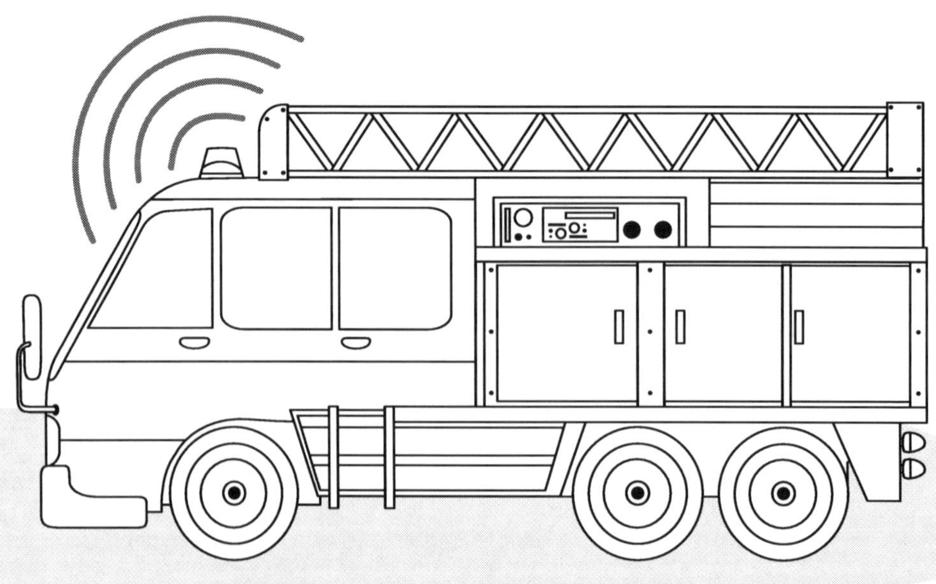

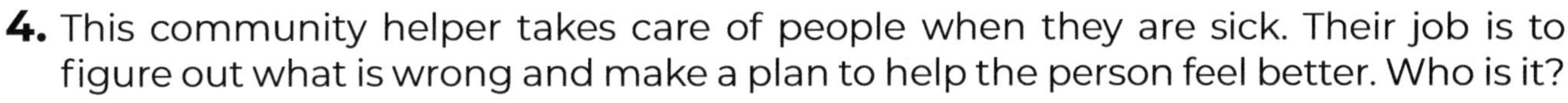

4. This community helper takes care of people when they are sick. Their job is to figure out what is wrong and make a plan to help the person feel better. Who is it?

....

....

5. This community helper loves children. Their job is to teach children to read and do math. Who is it?

....

....

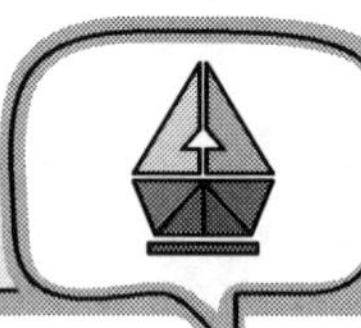

Yesterday you practiced matching community helpers with the job they do. Today you will choose a different community helper from the ones listed yesterday and explain what their job is.

Directions: Choose a community helper. On the lines below, explain what the community helper does in their job. Then, draw a picture of the person doing their job in the box below.

My Community Helper is a: ....

....

Their job is to: ....

....

....

You have spent several days learning, exploring, and explaining what community helpers do. Today, you will choose a community helper that you would like to know more about and use books or the internet to learn more about them and what they do.

1. What community helper do you want to know more about?

2. What does this person do in their job?

3. Would you like to do this job when you grow up?

A. Yes

B. No

4. Draw a picture of what this community helper does in the box below.

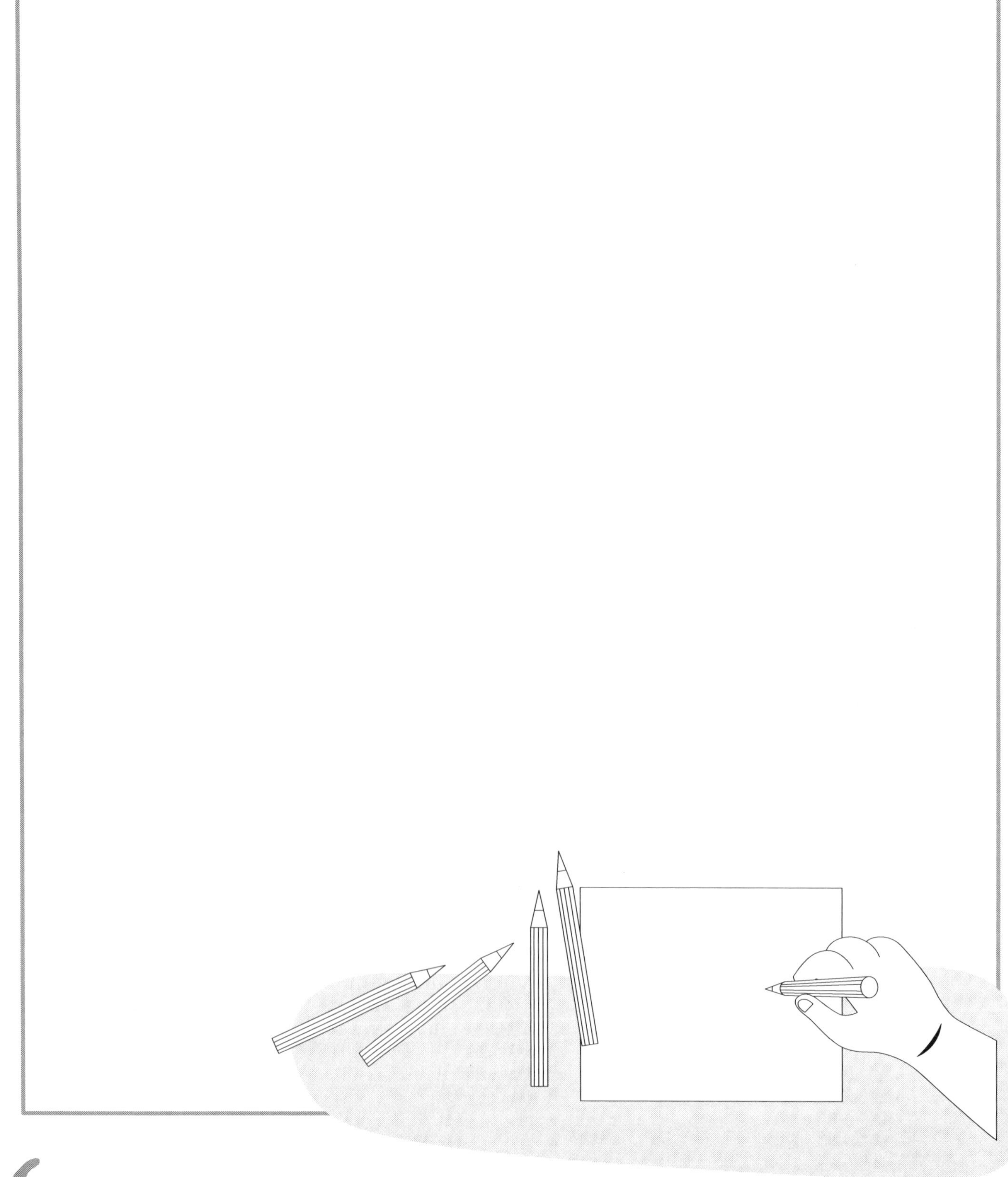

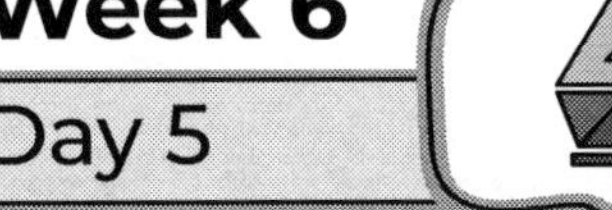

Yesterday you learned more about a community helper you were interested in. Today you will draw a picture of what you would like to be when you grow up.

Directions: What community helper would you like to be when you grow up? Draw a picture below.

WEEK 7

Civics and Government

The President of the United States

Identify and explain that the President of the United States is the leader of our country.

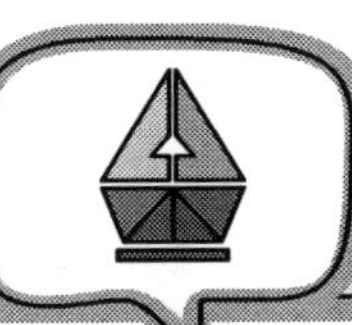

Directions: Read the text below. Then answer the questions that follow.

The President

The President of the United States of America is the leader of the country. They are responsible for making sure people follow the laws, or rules. The President is voted on by the citizens, or people, of the United States. They are allowed to serve the country for as long as 8 years. The President lives in the White House which is in Washington, D.C., our nation's capital.

1. The President of the United States:

A. Is the leader of the country
B. Makes sure people follow the laws
C. Both A and B

2. Who chooses the President of the United States?

A. People in government
B. The citizens, or people, of the United States
C. The President

3. How long is the President allowed to serve the country?

A. 2 years **C.** 6 years
B. 4 years **D.** 8 years

4. Where does the President live? Circle **all** correct answers.

A. The White House
B. Washington, D.C.
C. Their own house

Week 7 — The President of the United States

Day 2 — EXPLORING THE TOPIC

Yesterday you learned about the President of the United States. Today you will explore what the President does.

Directions: Read each description below. Decide whether or not it is something the President does. Write yes or no on the line.

1. The President helps to make sure the people of the United States follow the laws.

....

2. The President talks to the leaders of other countries.

....

3. The President is in charge of things like schools, libraries, and hospitals.

....

4. The President writes the laws, or rules, of our country.

....

5. The President helps to keep the people of the United States safe by deciding which rules should become laws.

....

Yesterday you learned about the different jobs of the President. Today you will explain what the President does in your own words.

Directions: Find out who the President of the United States is right now. Write a sentence or two to describe what you think the President does. Then, draw a picture to go with your sentence in the box below.

The President of the United States is: ....

....

....

Their job is to: ....

....

....

....

....

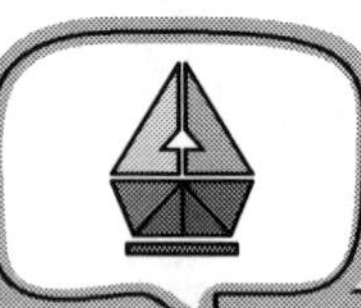

You have spent several days learning, exploring, and explaining what the President does. Today you will write about what you think it would be like to be the President.

I think being the President of the United States would be a (hard, easy) job because:

I (would, would not) like to be the President of the United States because:

Yesterday you learned more about what it would be like to be the President of the United States. Today you will write about and draw a picture of what you would do if you were the President.

Directions: Complete the sentence. Then draw a picture below.

If I were the President of the United States, I would:

WEEK 8

Civics and Government

The American Flag

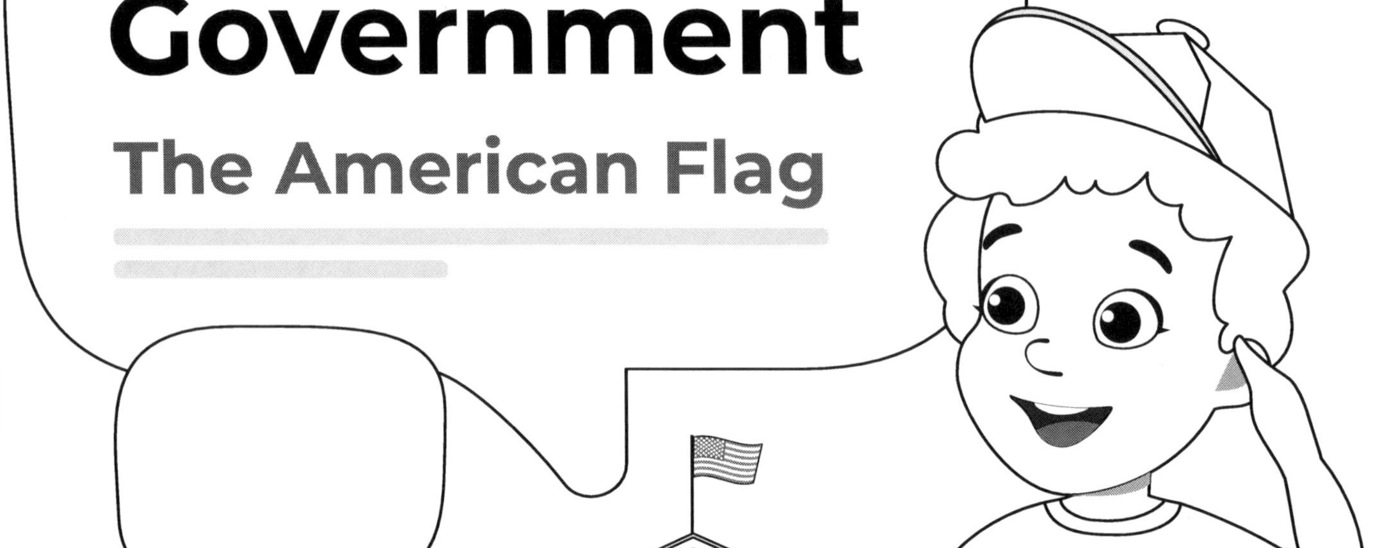

Learn and explore the importance of the American flag.

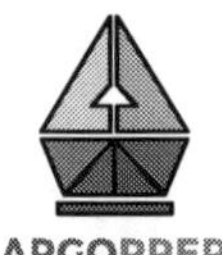

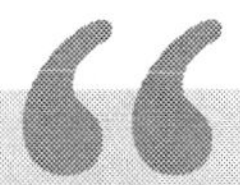

Directions: Read the text below. Then answer the questions that follow.

The American Flag

The American Flag is an important symbol of freedom in our country. The first American flag was sewn by a woman named Betsy Ross in 1776. The design of the flag has changed over time. Right now, the American flag has 13 red and white stripes to represent the 13 original colonies and 50 white stars that represent each state in America. Today flags are flown at many different places like schools, office buildings, and even homes. Where have you seen an American flag flying?.

1. The design of the American flag has always been the same.

A. True
B. False

2. The first flag was sewn over 200 years ago.

A. True
B. False

3. The 13 red and white stripes on a flag represent:

A. Different states
B. Freedom
C. The 13 Colonies
D. Nothing

4. Where are flags often flown? Circle all correct answers.

A. Schools
B. Offices
C. Homes

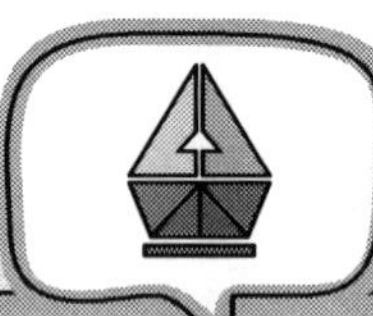

Yesterday you learned about the American flag. Today you will explore what the flag stands for.

The American flag is an important symbol in our country. A symbol is an object that represents something else. The flag is a **symbol** of freedom, strength, and unity. It reminds the American people of all the things that have happened in our country in the past to help us have the freedoms we have today. There are many other symbols of America besides the flag.

Directions: Read each word below. Decide whether or not it is a symbol of the United States of America. Write yes or no on the line.

1. The White House

2. Schools

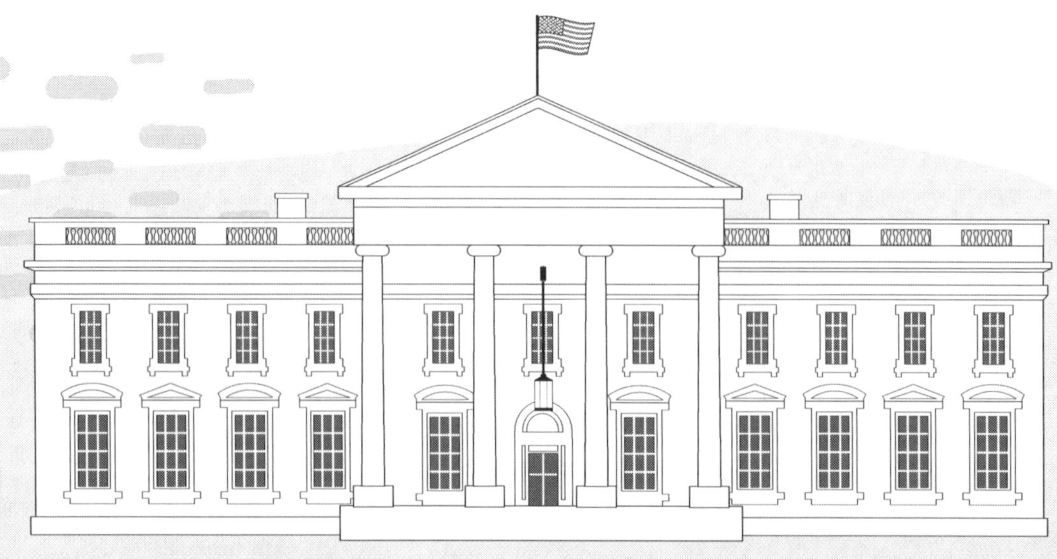

3. A Bald Eagle

4. The Statue of Liberty

5. Cars

Yesterday you learned about different symbols in our country. Today you will explain why the American flag is important to you.

Directions: Write a sentence or two to describe why the American flag is important to you. Then list 3 places you have seen the flag flying.

The American flag is important to me because:

3 places I have seen the American flag flying are:

1.
2.
3.

Week 8 The American Flag

You have spent several days learning about, exploring, and explaining why the American flag is important. Today, you will create your own drawing of the flag using the facts you have learned.

Directions: Using what you have learned about the stars and stripes of an American flag, draw a picture of the flag in the box below. Use the internet or books to help you, if needed.

The American Flag

ELABORATING ON THE TOPIC

Yesterday you drew a picture of the American flag. Today you will write about and draw a picture of another American symbol of your choice.

Directions: Complete the sentence. Then draw a picture of the symbol in the box.

....

.... is an important

American symbol because ....

....

....

....

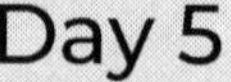

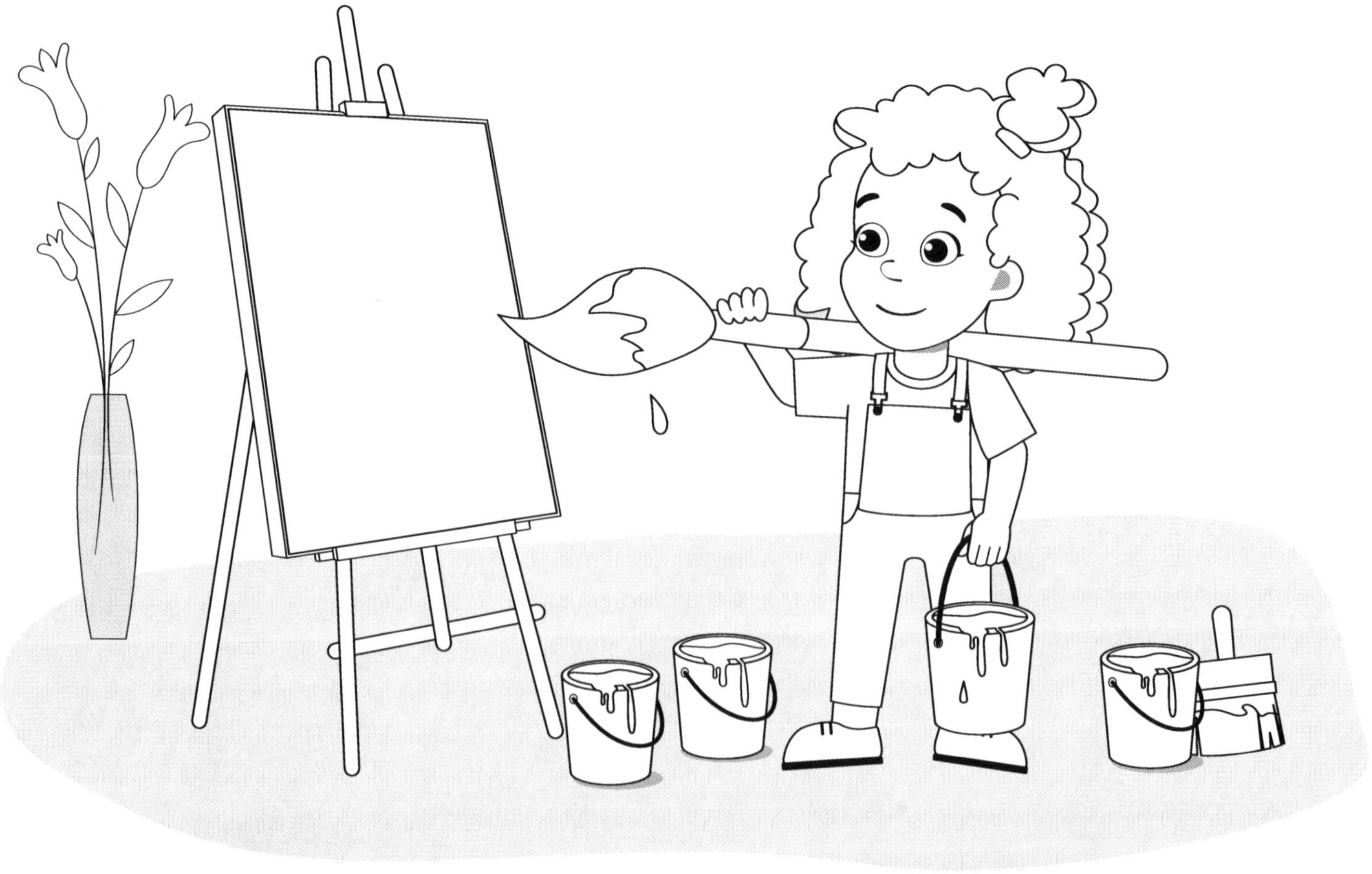

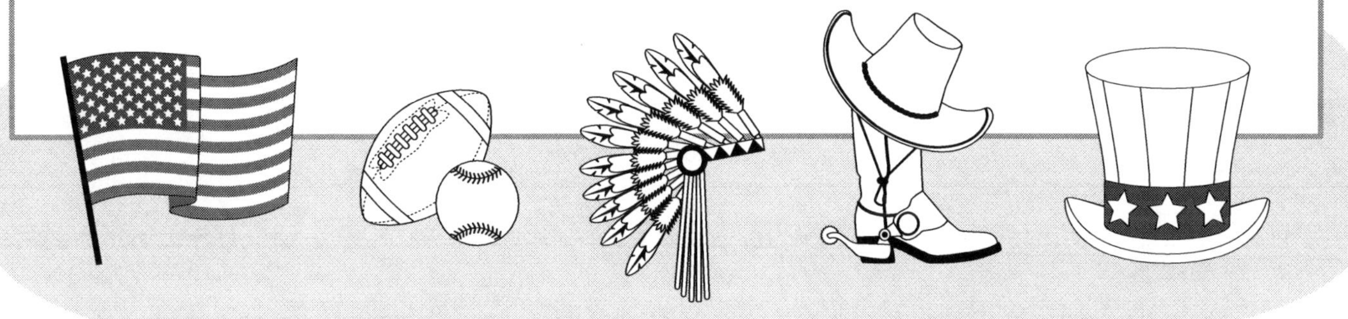

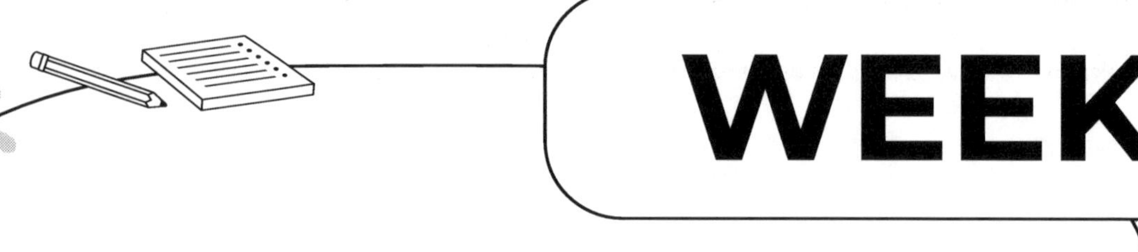

WEEK 9

Civics and Government

The Importance of Rules

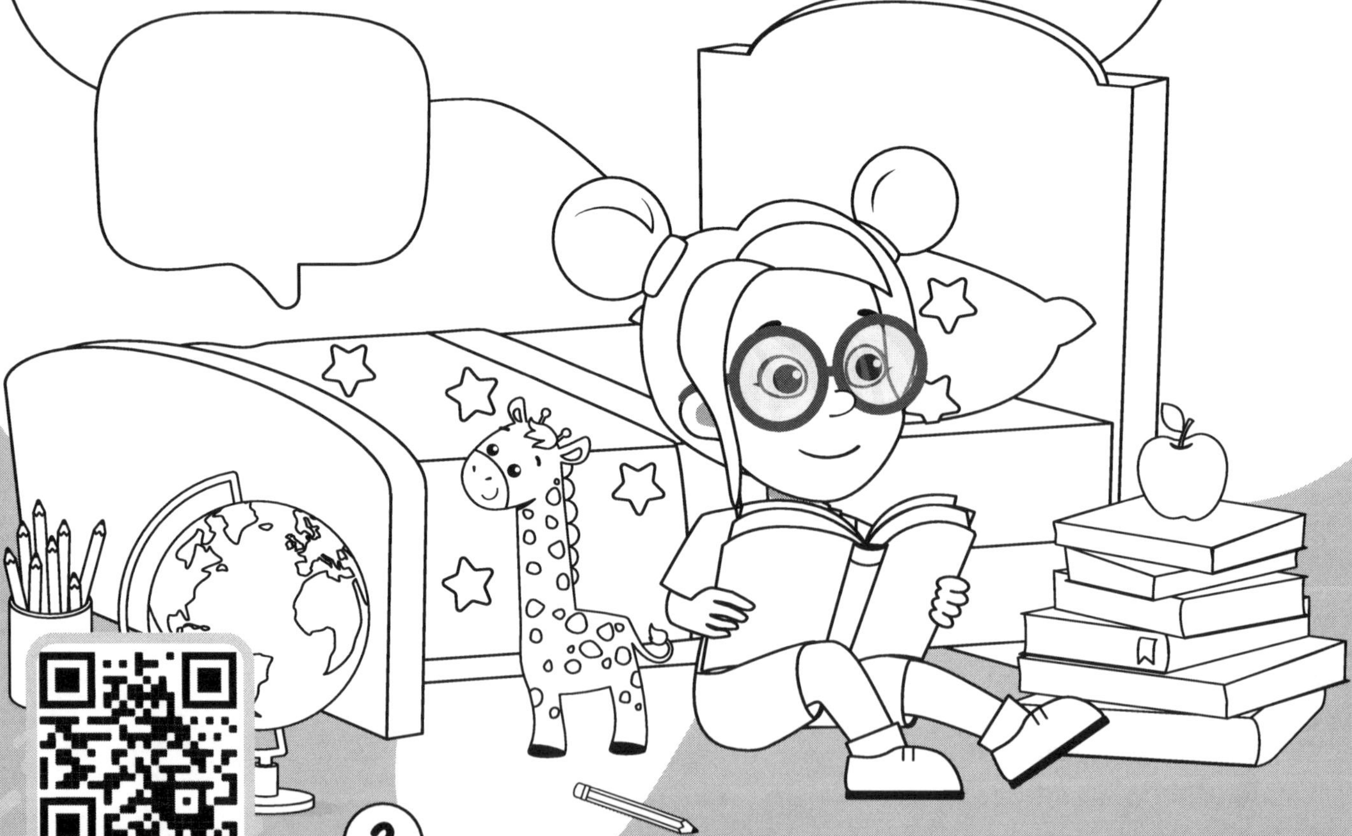

3

2 Explain the importance of following rules to ensure order and safety.

Directions: Read the text below. Then answer the questions that follow.

Why Do We Need Rules?

A **rule** is something you follow to keep yourself and others safe. You probably have rules at home and school. Can you think of other places that have rules? Rules are very similar to the laws we have in our state and country. Rules are important because they keep us safe and help ensure order. What do you think might happen if your classroom had no rules?

1. Rules and laws are very different.

A. True
B. False

2. Many different places have rules.

A. True
B. False

3. Rules are important because:

A. Teachers like to be in charge.
B. They keep us safe.
C. They are not important.

4. Your house and classroom have rules.

A. True
B. False

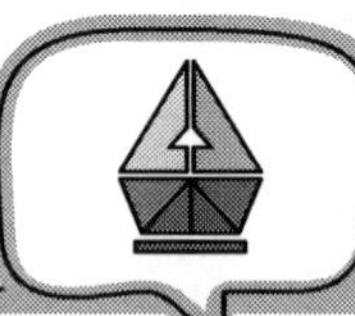

The Importance of Rules

EXPLORING THE TOPIC

Yesterday you learned about the importance of rules. Today you will explore different rules you have at home and school.

Directions: On the table below, list 3 rules you have to follow at home and 3 rules you have to follow at school.

Home	School

Week 9 — The Importance of Rules

Day 3 — EXPLAINING THE TOPIC

Yesterday you listed different rules you have to follow at home and school. Today you will explain why it is important to follow these rules.

Directions: Choose one rule from home and one rule from school. Complete the sentences below to explain why it is important to follow these rules.

Home Rule: ....

....

....

....

It is important to follow this rule because:

....

....

....

....

School Rule: ....

....

....

....

....

It is important to follow this rule because:

....

....

....

....

You have spent several days learning, exploring, and explaining why rules are important. Today you will create your own list of rules.

Directions: Using what you have learned about rules, create your own list of rules for your family. Write or draw them in the box below.

Yesterday you created your own list of rules. Today you will write about and draw a picture of what you have learned this week.

Directions: Complete the sentence.

Rules are important because ....

....

....

....

....

....

Week 9 — Day 5

The Importance of Rules

ELABORATING ON THE TOPIC

Directions: Draw a picture of what you look like when you are following the rules in your classroom.

WEEK 10

Civics and Government

Being a Good Citizen

Understand the importance of being a responsible member of a group.

Directions: Read the text below. Then answer the questions that follow.

What is a Citizen?

It is very important to be a good citizen. A **citizen** is a person who lives in a specific place. For example, all the people who live in New York are citizens of the state of New York. Being a citizen is similar to being part of a family or other group. Think about the different groups you are a part of. This could include your school, neighborhood, city, or church. Each of these groups probably has a set of rules that you must follow. Following these rules is an important part of being a responsible member of the group.

1. A citizen is a person who:

A. Is in a group
B. Lives in a specific place
C. Is responsible

2. You can only be a member of one group.

A. True
B. False

3. Being a responsible citizen or group member means following the rules.

A. True
B. False

4. Someone who lives in Boston, Massachusetts is a citizen of Boston AND a citizen of Massachusetts.

A. True
B. False

Week 10 — Being a Good Citizen

Day 2 — EXPLORING THE TOPIC

Yesterday you learned what it means to be a responsible citizen. Today you will explore your own citizenship.

Directions: Read each sentence below and fill in the blanks.

1. I am a citizen of ______________________________ .
   (neighborhood)

2. I am a citizen of ______________________________ .
   (city)

3. I am a citizen of ______________________________ .
   (state)

4. I am a citizen of ______________________________ .
   (country)

5. I am a citizen of ______________________________ .
   (continent)

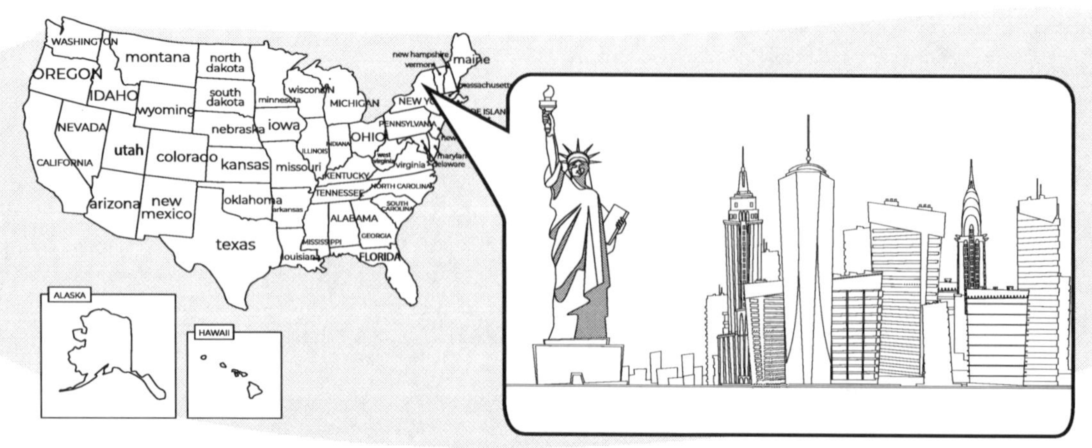

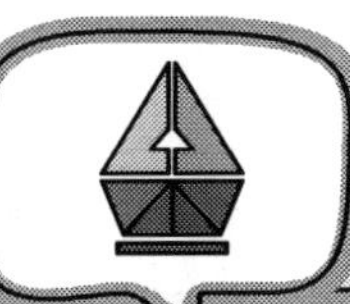

Week 10 Being a Good Citizen

Day 3 EXPLAINING THE TOPIC

Yesterday you listed the different places where you are a citizen. Today you will explain what it means to be a good citizen of these places.

Directions: Think about what it means to be a good citizen or a responsible member of a group. List as many ideas as you can think of on the table below.

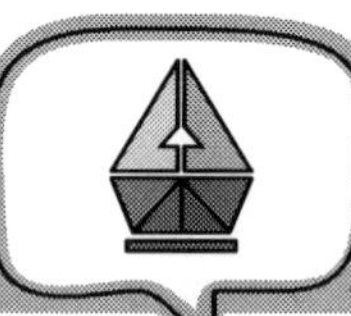

Being a Good Citizen

EXPLAINING THE TOPIC

You have spent several days learning, exploring, and explaining what it means to be a responsible citizen. Today you will write about why it is important to YOU to be a good citizen.

Directions: Complete the sentences below.

It is important to me to be a good citizen because: ....

....

....

....

....

I am a good citizen at school by: ....

....

....

....

....

I am a good citizen of my city or state by: ....

Being a Good Citizen

ELABORATING ON THE TOPIC

Yesterday you wrote about ways you show good citizenship. Today you will draw a picture of what being a good citizen might look like.

Directions: Draw a picture of what you look like when you are being a responsible citizen.

WEEK 11

Geography

Maps and Globes

Understand the difference between a map and a globe.

Directions: Read the text below. Then answer the questions that follow.

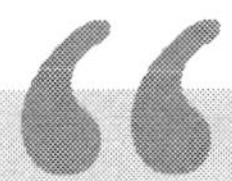

Maps and Globes

Maps and globes are important tools that help us understand the Earth and locate different places in our world. They are a little bit different, though. A **map** is a drawing of the Earth on a flat surface. It shows us where things like cities, countries, oceans, rivers, and forests are located. A **globe** is a drawing of the Earth on a sphere (like a ball). Globes show us the same types of features as a map.

1. Maps and globes are very similar.

A. True

B. False

2. A map is a drawing of the Earth on a .... surface.

A. Flat

B. Round

3. A globe is a drawing of the Earth on a .... surface.

A. Flat

B. Round

4. Which one shows cities, countries, oceans, rivers and forests?

A. A map

B. A globe

C. Both maps and globes

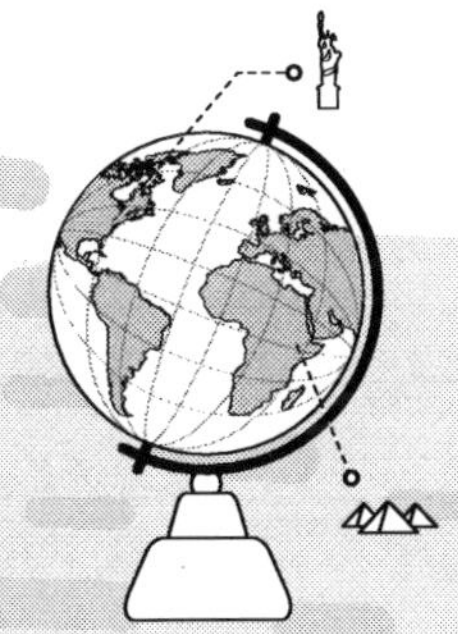

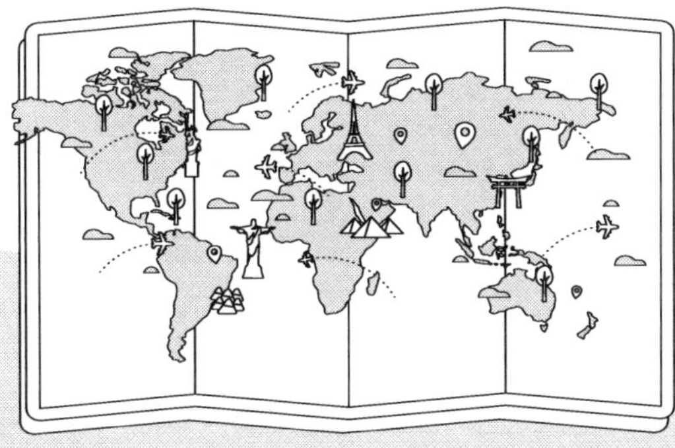

Yesterday you learned about maps and globes. Today you will further explore the things found on maps and globes.

Directions: Match each word and its definition below. Write the number on the table next to the correct word.

Continent	◯
Ocean	◯
River	◯
Highway	◯
Forest	◯

1. A long, flowing stream of water

2. A large solid area of land

3. An area of land with many trees

4. A large body of salt water

5. A main road

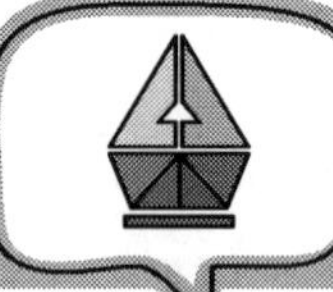

Maps and Globes

EXPLAINING THE TOPIC

Yesterday you learned more about map and globe features. Today you will explain how maps and globes are similar and different.

Directions: Think about what you have learned about maps and globes. On the table below, list the ways they are the same and different.

What is the same about maps and globes?	What is different about maps and globes?

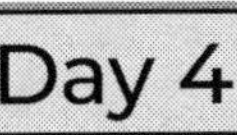

You have spent several days learning, exploring, and explaining the importance of maps and globes. Today you will create your own map for your house, neighborhood, or school.

Directions: Choose a place you know well. This might be your house, neighborhood, or school. Create a map of this place in the box below.

Yesterday you created a map of a place you know well. Today you will write about what you drew.

Directions: Complete the sentences below.

1. I created a map of my ....

....

2. The special features I included on my map are: ....

....

....

....

....

....

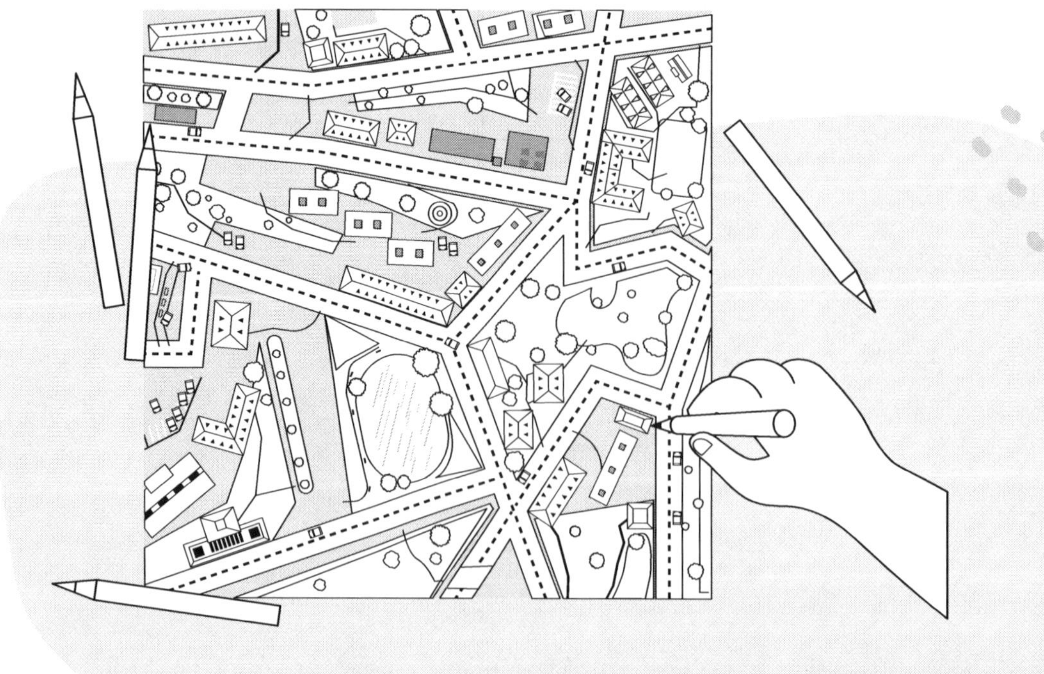

3. I know I created a map, not a globe, because:

WEEK 12

Geography

Addresses

Identify and describe the address of important places such as home or school.

Directions: Read the text below. Then answer the questions that follow.

What is an Address?

An **address** is a set of numbers, along with the name of a street, city, state, and zip code that tell exactly where a place is located. Every house and building has an address. This includes schools, hospitals, restaurants, and stores. It is very important to know the address where you live, in case there is ever an emergency. You should start practicing your street address now if you don't already know it!

1. An address includes:
   - **A.** Street and street number
   - **B.** City
   - **C.** State
   - **D.** All of the above
2. Restaurants do not have addresses.
   - **A.** True
   - **B.** False
3. Knowing the address where you live is very important.
   - **A.** True
   - **B.** False
4. An address tells:
   - **A.** How far away a place is
   - **B.** Exactly where a place is located
   - **C.** Who lives at a certain place

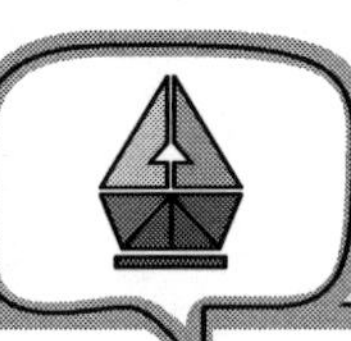

Addresses

EXPLORING THE TOPIC

Yesterday you learned about addresses. Today you will practice reading and writing your own address.

Directions: Read the example address below. Then have someone at home help you write your address on the lines below. After you have written your address, practice reading it several times. See if you are able to remember it without looking.

Pine Hill Elementary School

1234 Main Street

Springfield, Illinois 12345

Your Address:

....

....

....

....

Yesterday you practiced reading and writing your address. Today you will explain why it is important to know your address.

Directions: Complete the sentences below.

My address is: ....

....

....

It is important that I know my address because: ....

....

....

....

It is ok to give my address to the following people: ....

....

....

....

....

You have spent several days learning about, exploring, and explaining the importance of addresses. Today you will write the addresses for other important places.

Directions: Find out the addresses to the following places and write them below.

My School's Address

Address for the Nearest Library

Address for the Nearest Police or Fire Station

....

....

....

....

Yesterday, you wrote the addresses for important places nearby. Today you will practice saying your home address to 5 family members or close friends (with your parent's permission).

Directions: Complete the sentences below.

My address is:

....

....

....

....

I practiced saying my address to these people:

....

....

....

....

....

WEEK 13

Geography

Weather

Describe and give examples of seasonal weather.

ARGOPREP

Week 13 Weather

Day 1 ENGAGING WITH THE TOPIC

Directions: Read the text below. Then answer the questions that follow.

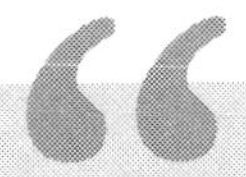

The Four Seasons

The four seasons are winter, spring, summer, and fall. The seasons change as the Earth orbits, or moves around, the sun. Each season lasts for about three months and has different types of weather. People dress differently and do different activities during each season, depending on what the weather is like. For instance, you can only ski in the winter when there is snow on the ground, and you would only want to go swimming outdoors when it is sunny and hot.

1. The seasons change as the Earth orbits the Sun.

A. True

B. False

2. Each season lasts about:

A. 2 months

B. 3 months

C. 4 months

D. 5 months

3. There are four different seasons.

A. True

B. False

4. Each season has different:

A. Weather

B. Popular activities

C. All of the above

Yesterday you learned some basic information about the four seasons. Today you will explore this concept by drawing pictures of the weather during each season.

Directions: Complete the table below by drawing a picture in each box showing what the weather is like during each of the four seasons where you live.

Winter	**Spring**
Summer	**Fall**

Yesterday you drew pictures that showed the weather during each of the four seasons where you live. Today you will write a sentence explaining what types of activities you like to do during each season.

Directions: Complete the sentences below.

In winter, I like to: ....

....

....

....

....

In spring, I like to: ....

....

....

....

....

....

In summer, I like to: ....

....

....

....

....

In fall, I like to: ....

....

....

....

....

You have spent several days learning, exploring, and explaining the differences between each of the four seasons. Today you will experiment with this content by drawing pictures of what people might wear during each season.

Directions: Complete the table below by drawing a picture in each box showing what people might wear during each of the four seasons where you live.

Winter	**Spring**
Summer	**Fall**

Yesterday you drew pictures that showed what people wear during each of the four seasons where you live. Today you will write a sentence to describe each of your pictures.

Directions: Complete the sentences below.

In winter, I wear: ....

....

....

....

....

In spring, I wear: ....

....

....

....

....

....

....

....

In summer, I wear: ....

....

....

....

....

In fall, I wear: ....

....

....

....

....

WEEK 14

Geography

Human Systems

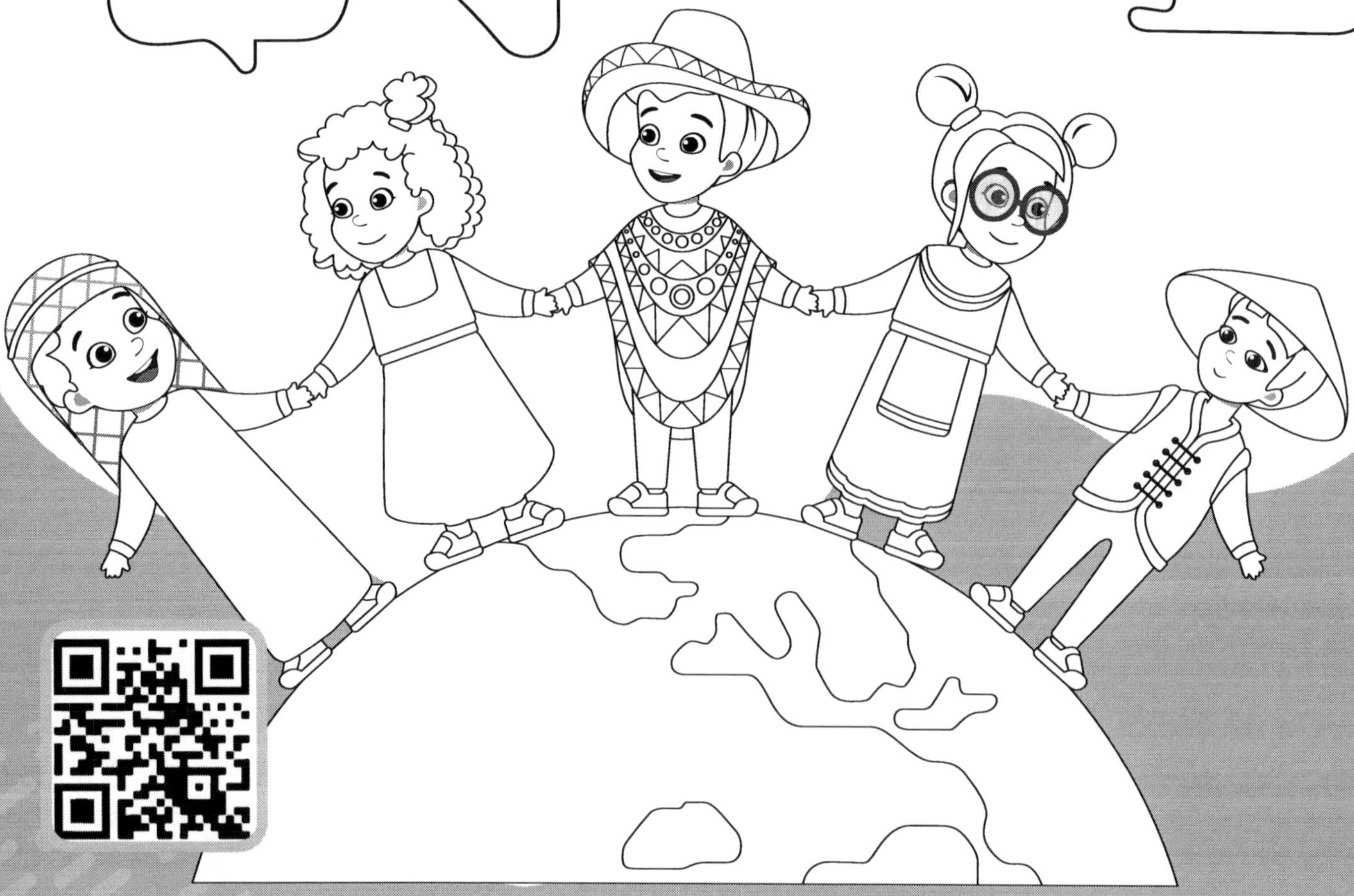

Identify and compare similarities and differences between families, classmates, neighbors, and cultural or ethnic groups.

Directions: Read the text below. Then answer the questions that follow.

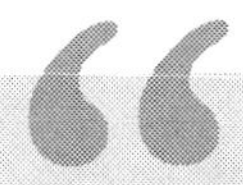

How are People Different?

Diverse is a word that means different, and people are different from one another. Think about all the people you know; your family, friends, neighbors, and classmates. How are they the same? How are they different? While there are probably many similarities among the people you know, their differences are what make them special.

1. Our differences make us special.

   A. True
   B. False

2. Diverse means:

   A. A group of people
   B. Same
   C. Different

3. All the people you know are exactly the same.

   A. True
   B. False

4. People that are different from you may include:

   A. Friends
   B. Neighbors
   C. Classmates
   D. All of the above

Yesterday you learned some basic information about how people are similar and different. Today you will explore this concept further.

Directions: Read the text below. Then answer the questions that follow.

People can be different in many ways. They may wear clothes that look different from yours, speak a different language or celebrate different holidays. Their food, music, and art may also be different from yours. We can learn a lot about other cultures, or groups of people, by studying the similarities and differences between us and asking questions.

1. List 5 ways people might be different.

A. ....

B. ....

C. ....

D. ....

E. ....

2. List 2 things you could do to learn more about another culture.

A. ....

B. ....

Yesterday you learned more about how people can be different. Today you will think of other things that may be different about diverse groups of people.

Directions: What are some other ways that diverse groups of people might be different? Complete the table below.

You have spent several days learning, exploring and explaining the differences between diverse groups of people. Today you will research a different culture to learn more about how it is similar and different from yours.

Directions: Choose a culture that is different from yours. Learn more about it by looking in books or on the internet. Then answer the questions below.

The group of people or culture I researched was:

Similarities	Differences

Yesterday you did research to learn more about another culture or group of people. Today you will draw pictures to show two main differences between your culture and the one you researched.

Directions: Choose two differences between your culture and the one you researched yesterday. Draw pictures below to show how they are different.

My Culture	....

WEEK 15

Geography

Improving Our Environment

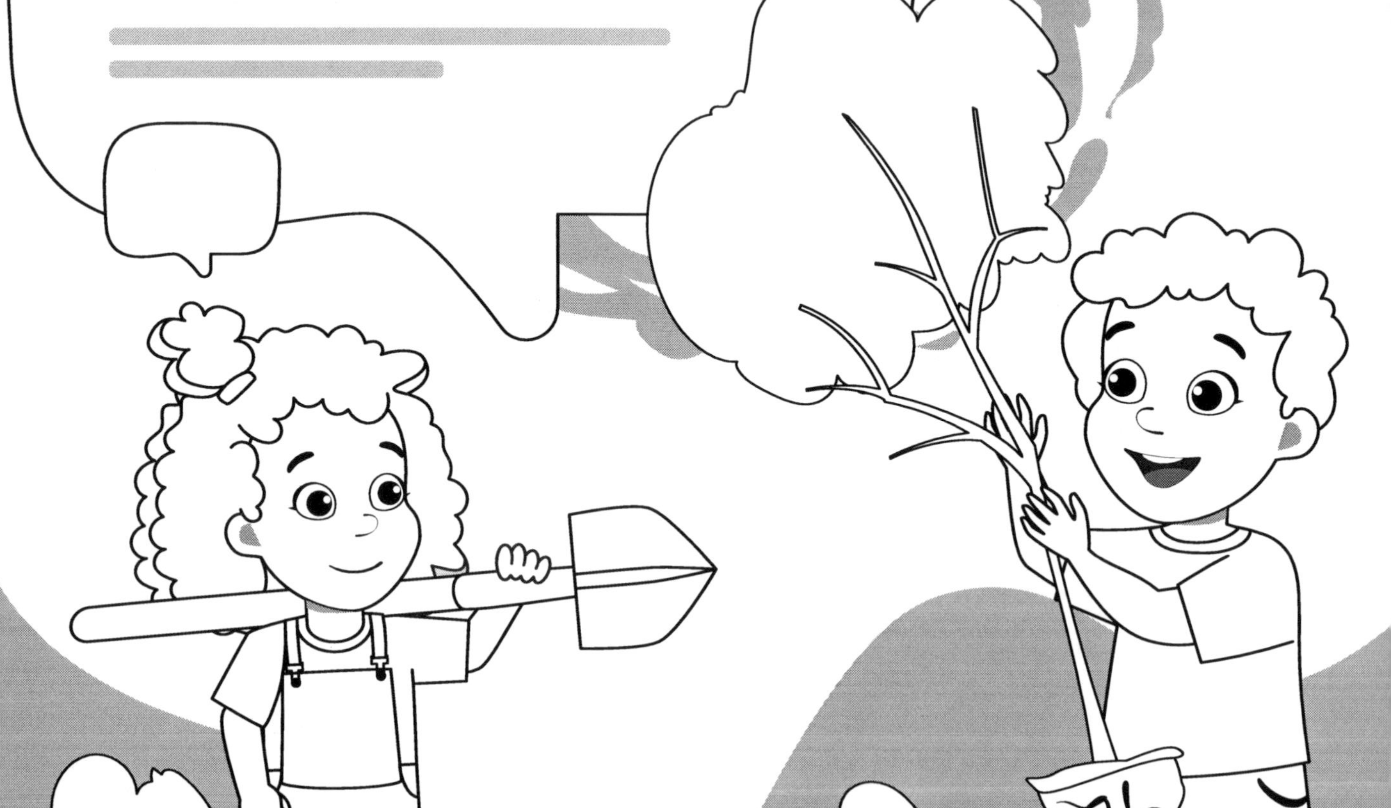

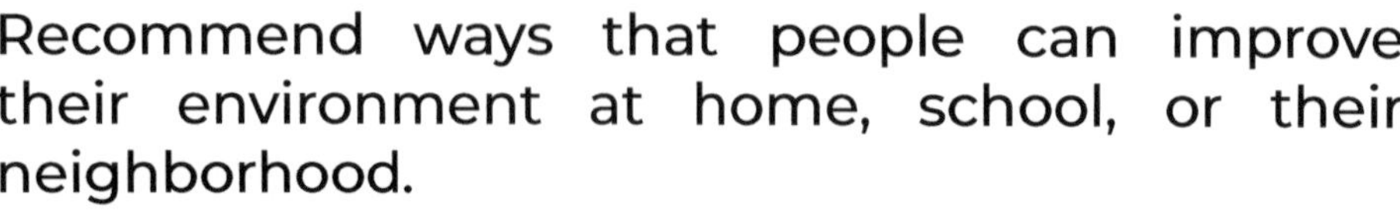
Recommend ways that people can improve their environment at home, school, or their neighborhood.

Week 15 Improving Our Environment

Day 1 ENGAGING WITH THE TOPIC

Directions: Read the text below. Then answer the questions that follow.

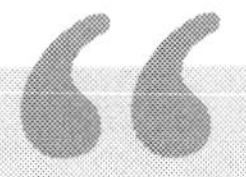

Our Environment

The **environment** is made up of all the living and nonliving things around us, including people, animals, and plants. It is important to take care of our environment so that all living things continue to thrive and grow. Sadly, some people do not care so much about the environment and do things that are harmful to plants and animals. Litter, single-use plastics, and pollution are all things that hurt our environment.

1. The environment is made up of:

A. People
B. Animals
C. Plants
D. All of the above

2. Trees are part of the environment.

A. True
B. False

3. To thrive means to take care of the environment.

A. True
B. False

4. Which are harmful to the environment? Circle all correct answers.

A. Planting a garden
B. Littering
C. A reusable water bottle
D. Air pollution

Yesterday you learned about the environment. Today you will further explore things that hurt our environment.

Directions: Read the text below. Then answer the questions that follow.

Many things that people do are harmful to our environment or can hurt living things. Littering rather than throwing away our trash, not recycling certain items, and polluting the air are all things that are harmful to plants, animals, and humans. There are even some things that we have to do as part of our daily lives that can be harmful to the environment. Many people have to drive cars to work or school, but cars can cause air pollution that is bad for the environment. What are other things that are harmful to the environment?

1. List 5 things that are not listed above that can hurt the environment.

A. ....

B. ....

C. ....

D. ....

E. ....

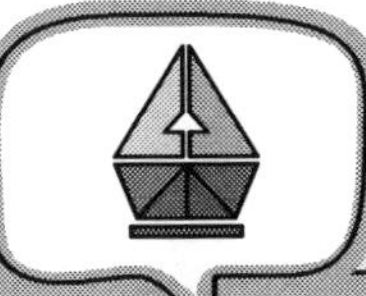

Improving Our Environment

EXPLAINING THE TOPIC

Yesterday you learned more about things that are harmful to the environment. Today you will choose one of those things and explain why it is harmful to the environment.

Directions: Complete the sentence below. Then, draw a picture that matches your sentence.

....

is harmful to the environment because: ....

....

....

....

....

....

Week 15 — Improving Our Environment

Day 4 — EXPERIENCING THE TOPIC

You have spent several days learning, exploring, and explaining how certain things are harmful to the environment. Today you will think of ways to improve the environment.

Directions: What are things that can be done to improve the environment or make it better? Complete the table below with your ideas.

Improving Our Environment

ELABORATING ON THE TOPIC

Yesterday you listed ways to improve the environment. Today you will choose one item from yesterday's list to complete.

Directions: Choose one item from yesterday's list to complete. Then, write a sentence below, describing what you did and how it was helpful to the environment. Then draw a picture that matches your sentence.

To improve the environment, I ....

....

....

....

This is helpful because: ....

....

....

....

WEEK 16

Economics

Wants and Needs

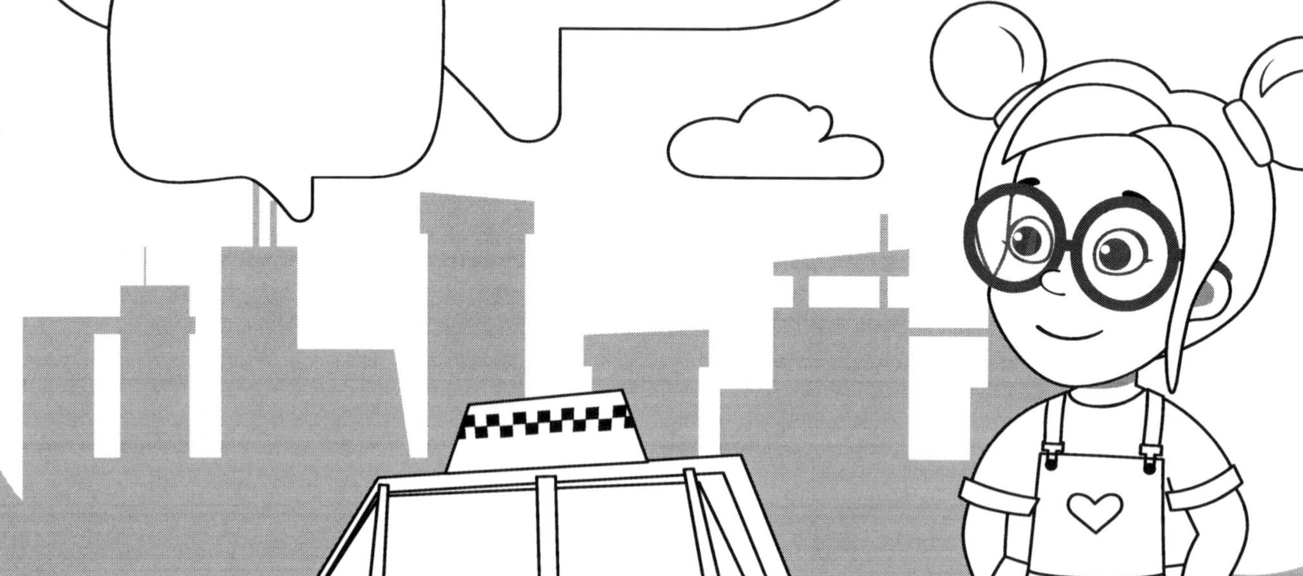

Describe the difference between wants and needs.

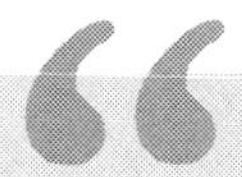

Wants and Needs

ENGAGING WITH THE TOPIC

Directions: Read the text below. Then answer the questions that follow.

Wants and Needs

People work to earn money to buy the things they want and need. Wants and needs are different. **Needs** are the things necessary to live and be safe and healthy. These would include a house, clothing, food, and transportation. **Wants** are the extra things people like to have for fun. Examples of wants include toys and games, vacations, and visits to zoos, museums, and restaurants. It is important to take care of our needs before our wants.

1. Which one should be taken care of first?

A. Wants
B. Needs
C. Neither
D. Both

2. Wants are necessary for living a healthy, safe life.

A. True
B. False

3. Food, shelter, and clothing are all examples of needs.

A. True
B. False

4. Visiting a restaurant is an example of a:

A. Want
B. Need

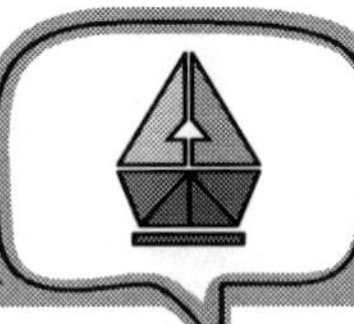

Wants and Needs

EXPLORING THE TOPIC

Yesterday you learned about wants and needs. Today you will further explore your own wants and needs.

Directions: On the table below, list your own wants and needs based on what you learned yesterday.

Wants	Needs

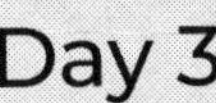

Wants and Needs

EXPLAINING THE TOPIC

Yesterday you listed your own wants and needs. Today you will choose one of those things and explain why it is a want or need.

Directions: Complete the sentence below. Then draw a picture that matches your sentence.

I (want/need): ....

I know this is a (want/need) because: ....

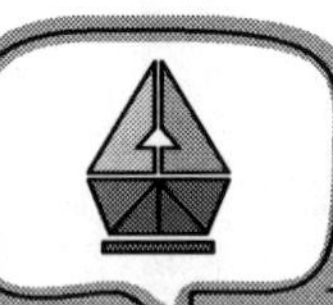

Wants and Needs

EXPERIENCING THE TOPIC

You have spent several days learning, exploring, and explaining the difference between wants and needs. Today you will read a passage and identify the characters' wants and needs.

Directions: Read the passage. Then, record Suzi's wants and needs on the table below.

Suzi just moved to a new house in a different city. She also has a new job as a teacher. Suzi must find a new apartment to live in, as well as some furniture to put in it. Suzi is so excited to start exploring her new city. When she has a few days off work, she would like to visit some museums and restaurants that she read about. Before she starts her new job, Suzi must go shopping to buy clothes that she can wear to work. She decides to take a taxi downtown to start shopping.

What are Suzi's wants? What are her needs? List them below.

Wants	Needs

Yesterday you identified the wants and needs of a character in a passage. Today you reflect on what you've learned this week.

Directions: Using the passage from yesterday, complete the sentences below.

The first thing I think Suzi should buy is ....

....

....

I think this because: ....

....

....

....

....

I don't think Suzi should spend money on ....

....

....

because ....

....

....

....

TAXI

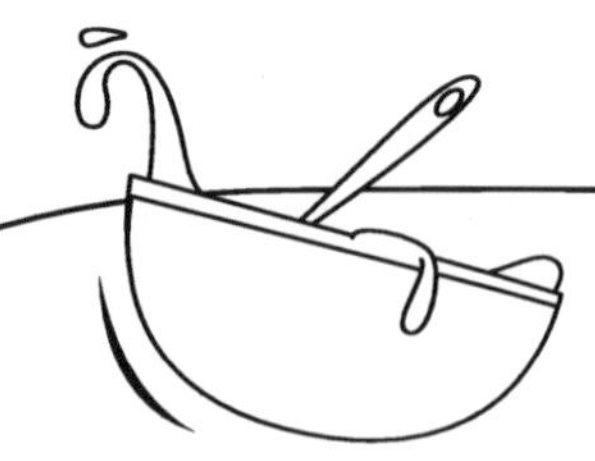

WEEK 17

Economics

Jobs - Part 1

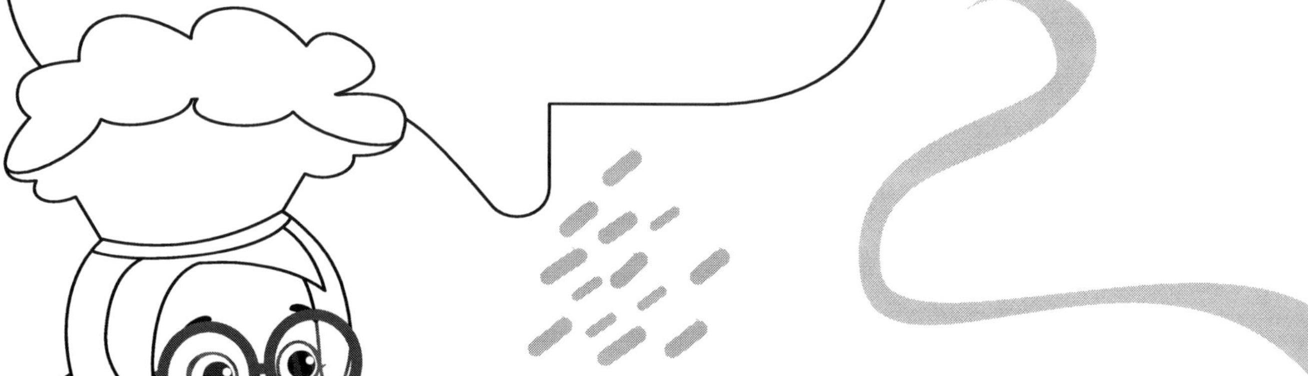

Identify and describe different types of jobs people do.

Directions: Read the text below. Then answer the questions that follow.

What is a Job?

A **job** is the work someone does on a regular basis to earn money. There are many different types of jobs people can do. Some jobs require workers to go to college or have special training to learn the skills needed for the job. Some jobs require workers to have or use special tools or materials. Workers get paid to do their job. This is how people earn money to pay for their wants and needs.

1. What is a job?

   A. College classes
   B. Special training
   C. Work
   D. Special tools

2. You may need to go to college to do certain types of jobs.

   A. True
   B. False

3. Workers do not get paid for doing their job.

   A. True
   B. False

4. Some jobs require:

   A. College
   B. Special training
   C. Special tools or materials
   D. All of the above

Yesterday you learned what a job is. Today you will further explore the types of jobs people have.

There are many different types of jobs. Some people have jobs helping or caring for other people. These jobs would include being a doctor, nurse, or teacher. Some people have jobs providing services like plumbers, hairdressers and mechanics. Other people have jobs running businesses such as grocery stores, restaurants, and laundromats. What other jobs can you think of?

Directions: On the table below, list as many jobs as you can think of. You may also draw pictures of the jobs.

What jobs can you think of?

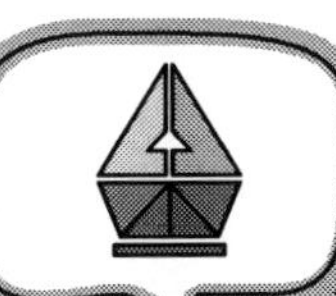

Week 17 — Jobs - Part I

Day 3 — EXPLAINING THE TOPIC

Yesterday you listed different jobs. Today you will choose one of the jobs and explain what that person does each day.

Directions: Complete the sentence below. Then draw a picture that matches your sentence.

Job: ....

....

A .... job is to ....

....

....

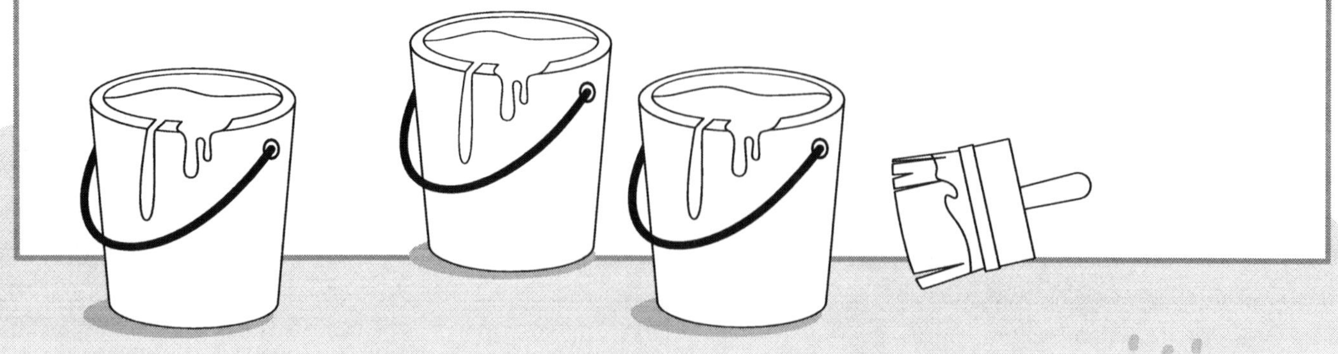

You have spent several days learning, exploring, and explaining different jobs. Today you will read passages and figure out what the character's job is.

Directions: Read each passage. Then decide what job the character has and write it on the line.

1. Jacobi works with kids all day. He helps them learn their letters and numbers. He also teaches them songs and does activities with them. What is Jacobi's job?

....

....

2. Sarah serves food to people. She makes sure they have fun and get everything they order. What is Sarah's job?

....

....

3. Ezra builds roads and highways. He usually operates the excavator at the worksite. What is Ezra's job?

....

....

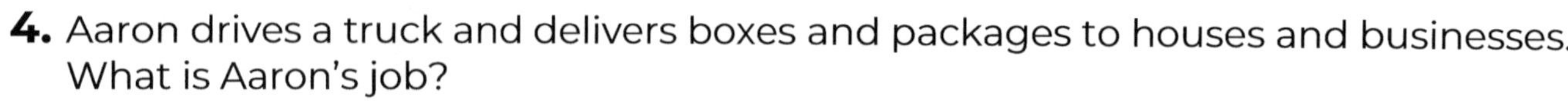

4. Aaron drives a truck and delivers boxes and packages to houses and businesses. What is Aaron's job?

....

....

5. Jamal makes breads, cookies, and cakes and sells them to customers at the farmer's market. What is Jamal's job?

....

....

Jobs - Part I

ELABORATING ON THE TOPIC

Yesterday, you identified the job of a character in a passage. Today you will write about the job you would like to have when you grow up.

Directions: Complete the sentence below. Then draw a picture that matches your sentence.

When I grow up, I would like to be a ....

....

....

because

....

....

....

WEEK 18

Economics

Jobs - Part 2

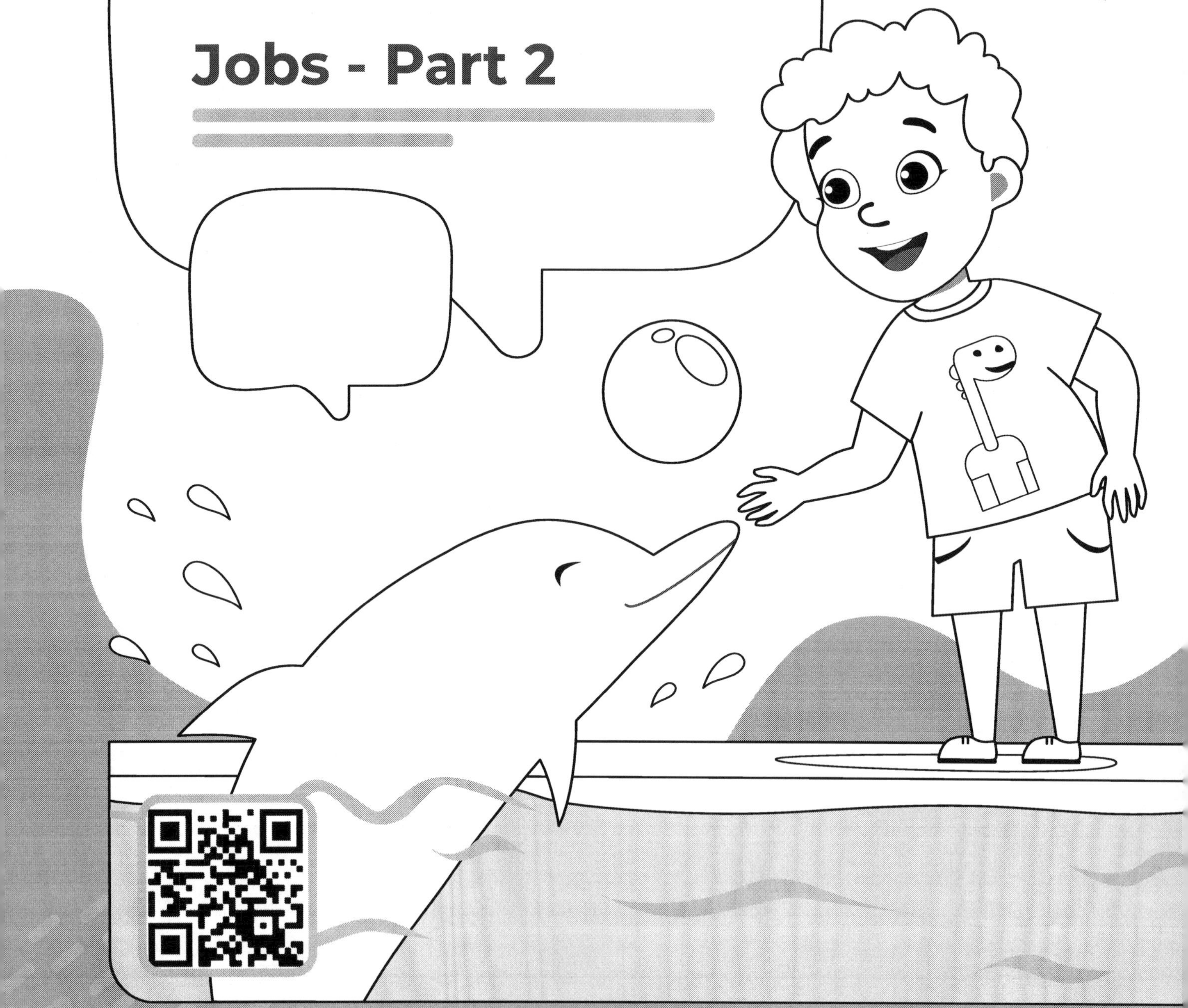

Identify and describe the tools or equipment used in different types of jobs.

Directions: Read the text below. Then answer the questions that follow.

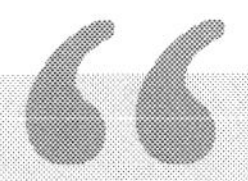

What Tools Do You Need?

Many jobs require workers to use certain tools or equipment. Often, workers have to do training to learn how to safely and properly operate these tools. For instance, construction workers use a lot of different types of vehicles and equipment to build houses, roads, and buildings. It is important they know how to operate the equipment the right way to keep themselves and others safe. Can you think of other workers that use special tools or equipment?

1. Many jobs require (circle all that apply):

A. Special equipment
B. Special training
C. Sleep
D. Special tools

2. You do not need training to operate special tools and equipment.

A. True
B. False

3. Learning to operate equipment the right way keeps people safe.

A. True
B. False

4. Construction workers use a lot of special equipment in their job.

A. True
B. False

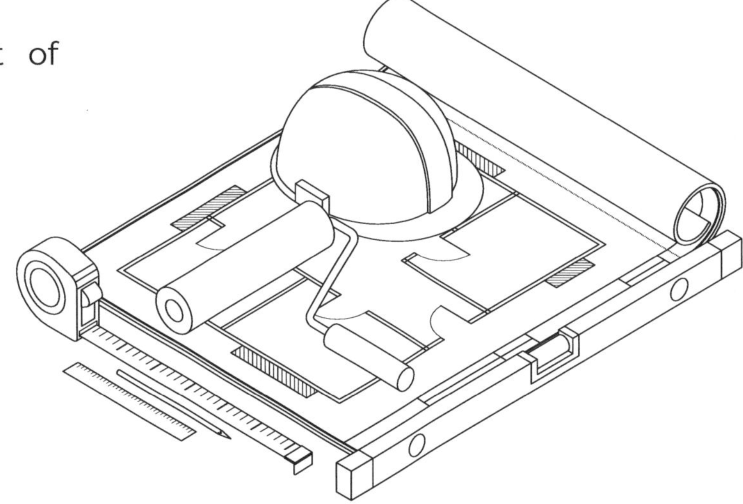

Jobs - Part 2

EXPLORING THE TOPIC

Yesterday you learned about the special equipment some workers use. Today you will further explore the types of jobs that require equipment.

There are many different types of workers that use tools and equipment. Construction workers use many different vehicles like excavators, backhoes, and cranes. Firefighters use ladder trucks and long hoses. Artists use paintbrushes, clay, and canvases. What other workers can you think of that use special tools?

Directions: On the table below, list as many jobs as you can think of, as well as the equipment or tools people use to do that job. You may also draw pictures of the jobs.

Job	Equipment or Tools Needed

Week 18 — Jobs - Part 2

Day 3 — EXPLAINING THE TOPIC

Yesterday you listed different jobs and the equipment or tools needed for each one. Today you will choose one of the jobs you listed and explain how a worker might use the tools needed for the job.

Directions: Complete the sentence below. Then draw a picture that matches your sentence.

Job: ....

....

How they use tools: ....

....

....

....

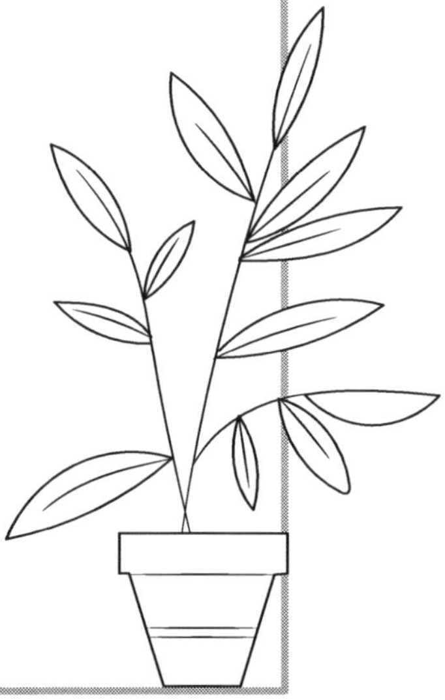

You have spent several days learning about, exploring, and explaining different jobs and equipment. Today you will read passages and match the character's job to the tools he or she needs.

Directions: Read each passage. Then decide which tools the character needs. Write the correct letter on the line.

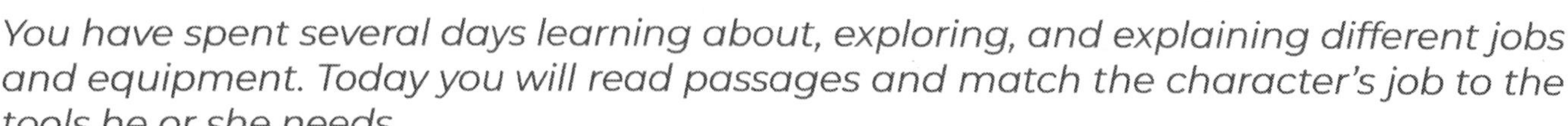

A. Bowls, mixer, spatula	**B. Wetsuit, whistle, fish**
C. Paper, pencils, computer	**D. Car lift, batteries, tires**

1. Joe is a mechanic. People bring their cars to him to fix when they are broken. What tools does Joe need for his job?

2. Kai is a baker. She makes beautiful cakes for people's birthdays and other celebrations. What tools does Kai need for her job?

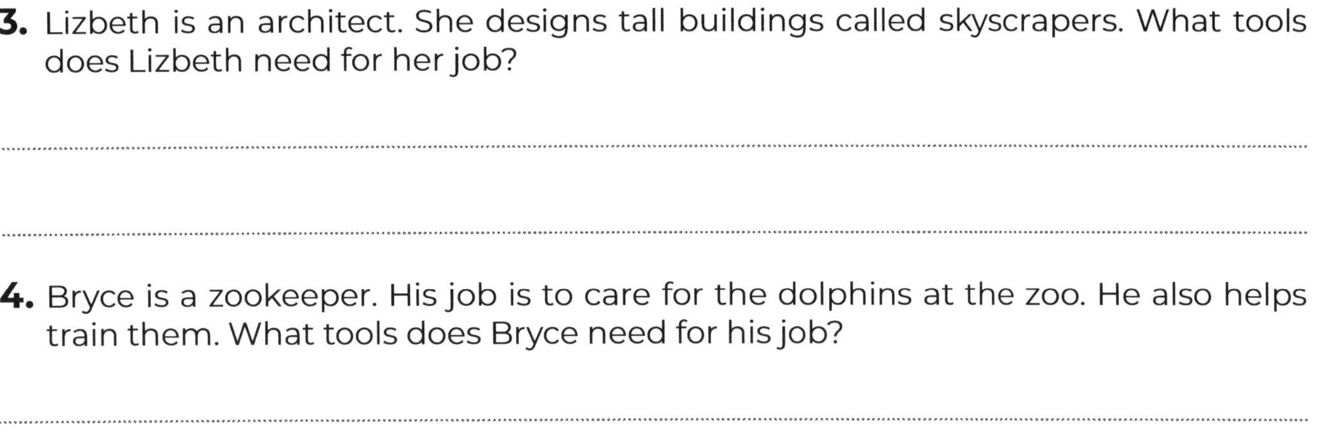

3. Lizbeth is an architect. She designs tall buildings called skyscrapers. What tools does Lizbeth need for her job?

....

....

4. Bryce is a zookeeper. His job is to care for the dolphins at the zoo. He also helps train them. What tools does Bryce need for his job?

....

....

Yesterday you identified the tools needed by characters in passages. Today you will write about the job you would like to have when you grow up and the tools you might need.

Directions: Complete the sentence below. Then draw a picture that matches your sentence.

When I grow up, I would like to be a ....

....

....

....

To do this job, I might need: ....

....

....

WEEK 19

Economics

Choosing a Job

Explain why people in a community choose different jobs.

Directions: Read the text below. Then answer the questions that follow.

How Do People Choose Jobs?

There are many different types of jobs. You may wonder how people choose which job they want to do. Some people choose jobs because they are really good at something. For instance, someone who is really good at painting may choose to become an artist. Other people choose jobs because it is something they really like to do. For instance, someone who loves to play basketball may choose to become a basketball coach at a school. What job do you think you will choose?

1. People choose jobs because: (choose all that apply)

A. They are good at something.
B. They really dislike something.
C. They enjoy doing something.
D. None of the above

2. There are many different jobs to choose from.

A. True
B. False

3. You should choose a job doing something you dislike.

A. True
B. False

4. Someone who likes animals may choose to become:

A. A shop owner
B. A zookeeper
C. A doctor
D. A mechanic

Yesterday you learned how people choose jobs. Today you will further explore this concept.

Directions: Read each passage. Then decide which job the character might choose to do. Write the correct letter on the line.

A. **Park ranger**	B. **Architect**
C. **Math teacher**	D. **Chef**

1. Ray loves building with blocks. He is really good at building tall towers and neat buildings. What job might Ray choose?

....

2. Tim really likes children and is very good at math. What job might Tim choose?

....

3. Marcela really enjoys trying new foods. Her family and friends always love trying out the new recipes she makes. What job might Marcela choose?

4. Carrie likes to be outside in nature. She also enjoys teaching others about bugs, trees, and small animals. What job might Carrie choose?

Choosing a Job

EXPLAINING THE TOPIC

Yesterday you matched jobs with characters in passages. Today you will explain how people might choose their job.

Directions: Complete the sentence below. Then draw a picture that matches your sentence.

People choose certain jobs because ....

....

....

....

Week 19 — Choosing a Job

Day 4 — EXPERIENCING THE TOPIC

You have spent several days learning, exploring, and explaining how people choose jobs. Today you will list things you like doing and are good at.

Directions: Complete the table below with things you like and things you are good at.

Things You Like Doing	Things You Are Good At

Yesterday you identified the things you like doing and are good at. Today, using that list, you will write about the job you might choose when you grow up.

Directions: Complete the sentence below. Then, draw a picture that matches your sentence.

When I grow up, I might choose to be a ....

....

....

because ....

....

....

....

WEEK 20

Economics

Working at Home

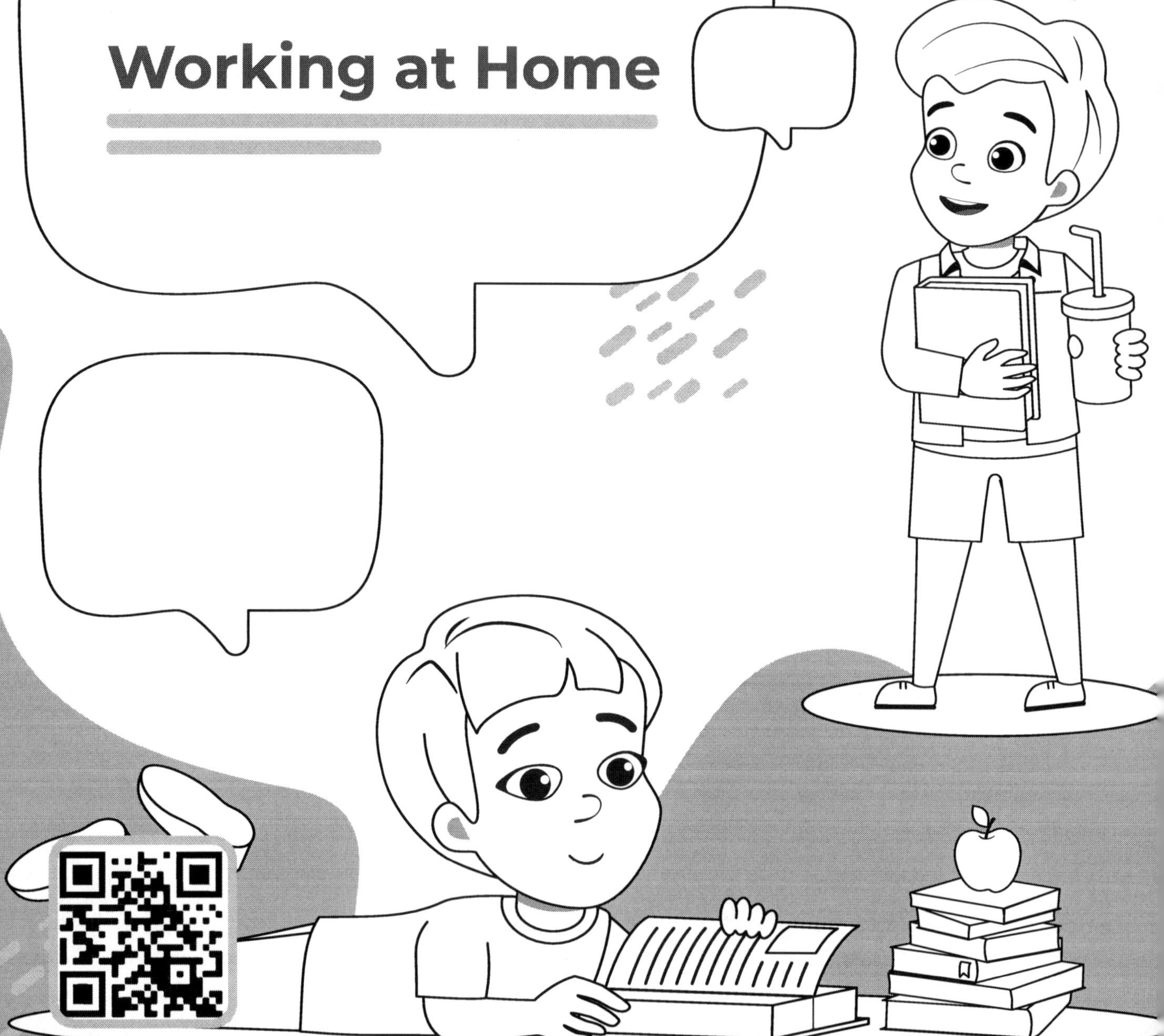

Give examples of work activities people do at home.

Directions: Read the text below. Then answer the questions that follow.

Working at Home

Working at home can mean many different things. Some people have an office in their home and do their job there. Other people do different kinds of work at home such as caring for their family or homeschooling young children. Doing chores around the house is another way people do work at home. What kinds of work do you do at your house?

1. Working at home might include:

A. Caring for children
B. Doing chores
C. Doing a job
D. All of the above

2. Working at home can mean many different things.

A. True
B. False

3. People are not able to do jobs from their home.

A. True
B. False

4. Kids can do work at home.

A. True
B. False

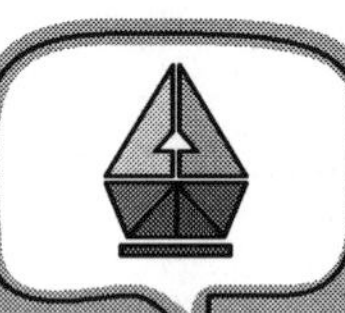

Week 20 — Working at Home

Day 2 — EXPLORING THE TOPIC

Yesterday you learned how people work at home. Today you will further explore this concept by deciding which jobs can be done at home and which cannot.

Directions: Read each job below. Decide if it can be done at home. Write it on the table below in the correct column.

Cleaning the bathroom	Making phone calls	Seeing patients	Caring for zoo animals
Stocking grocery store shelves	Teaching children	Driving a bus	Doing homework

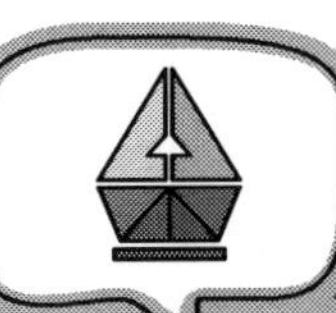

Working at Home

EXPLORING THE TOPIC

Yes	No

Yesterday you decided which jobs could be done from home. Today you will explain how people might do certain jobs at home.

Directions: Choose one of the jobs you listed in the "yes" column on yesterday's assignment. Complete the sentence below. Then, draw a picture that matches your sentence.

People can .... from home.

....

I know this because ....

....

You have spent several days learning, exploring, and explaining how people work at home. Today you will list things you do at home.

Directions: Complete the table below with things you do at your house.

What work do you do at your house?

Yesterday you identified the things you do to work at your house. Today using that list, you will write about one of the jobs you do at your house.

Directions: Complete the sentence below. Then draw a picture that matches your sentence.

At my house, I do work at home by ....

....

....

....

....

....

ANSWER
KEYS
ARGOPREP

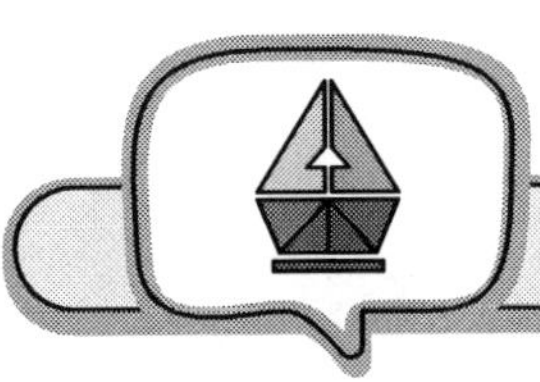

Answer Key

Week 1

Day 1

1. True
2. D
3. False

Day 2

Same:	Different
Tools	Clothing
	Houses
	Toy and Games
	Food
	Transportation

Day 3

1. Answers will vary. (Examples may include: bonnets, long dresses, pants with suspenders, work boots)
2. Answers will vary. (Examples may include: outdoor games, cards, games played with a ball)
3. Answers will vary. (Examples may include: small huts, teepees, small homes with lanterns or wood-burning stoves)

Day 4

1. Answers will vary. (Examples may include: sticks, straws of wheat)
2. Answers will vary.
3. Answers will vary.

Day 5

1. Answers will vary. (Examples might include: hunting for food, reading books)
2. Answers will vary. (Examples might include: playing on a tablet, going to a restaurant)
3. Answers will vary.

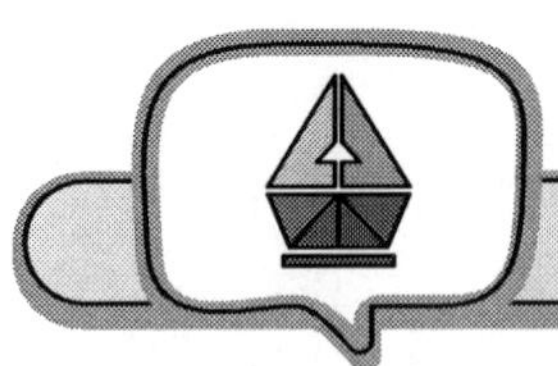

Week 2

Day 1

1. True
2. B
3. C

Day 2

Beliefs	Actions
Equal Rights	Gave Speeches
Peace and Kindness	Led Protests
Able to Vote	Inspired Others

Day 3

1. Answers will vary. (Examples may include: He fought for equal rights. He thought everyone should be treated equally.)

Day 4

All answers will vary. (Examples may include: complete acts of kindness in his honor, write a letter to your school principal about a rule you don't think is fair)

Day 5

1. Answers will vary. (Examples might include: It's important to celebrate important people from our country's history because they worked so hard to make our country better.)
2. Answers will vary. (Examples might include: George Washington, Rosa Parks, Barack Obama)
3. Answers will vary.

Week 3

Day 1

1. False
2. D
3. D

Day 2

Yes	No
Fireworks	Egg Hunt
Picnic	Trick or Treating
Parade	Decorating a Tree

Day 3

1. Answers will vary. (Examples may include: It is our country's birthday. It is when our country became free.)

Day 4

All answers will vary. (Examples may include: going to a parade in town, setting off fireworks with neighbors)

Day 5

1. Answers will vary. (Examples might include: It's important to celebrate important events from our country's history because they mark important dates like our nation's birthday.)
2. Answers will vary. (Examples might include: Memorial Day, Veteran's Day)
3. Answers will vary.

Week 4

Day 1

1. B
2. D
3. D

Day 2

1. 1, 2, 3, 4, 5
2. A, B, C, D, E
3. 1:00, 2:00, 3:00, 4:00, 5:00

Day 3

1. Answers will vary. (Examples may include: Sequencing is important because numbers and letters have to be in a specific order so we're not confused.)

Day 4

Answers will vary. (Examples may include: reading 9:00, math 10:30, lunch 11:30, recess 12:00, gym 12:30, spanish 1:30, writing 2:30)

Day 5

Answers will vary.

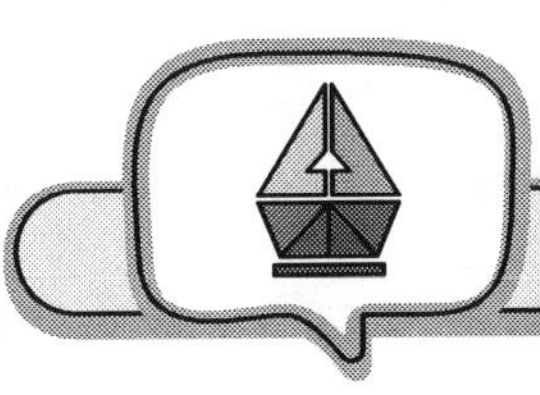

Week 5

Day 1

1. B
2. D
3. A

Day 2

1. Sunday, Monday, Tuesday, Wednesday, Thursday, Friday, Saturday
2. January, February, March, April, May, June, July, August, September, October, November, December

Day 3

1. Answers will vary. (Examples may include: Valentine's Day, 4th of July, Christmas)
2. Answers will vary. (Examples may include: first day of summer, full moon, first day of winter)
3. Answers will vary.

Day 4

Answers will vary. (Examples may include: birthdays, first/last day of school, vacation)

Day 5

Answers will vary.

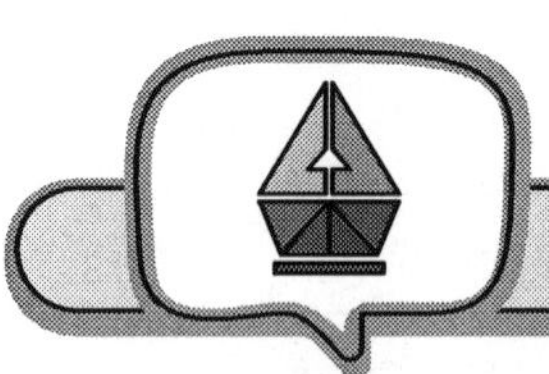

Week 6

Day 1

1. C
2. D
3. C

Day 2

1. Librarian
2. Veterinarian
3. Firefighter
4. Doctor or nurse
5. Teacher

Day 3

Answers will vary. (Examples will be similar to the descriptions given in the activity from Day 2)

Day 4

Answers will vary. (Example: I want to learn more about a police officer. I found out that a police officer is in charge of protecting people and making sure people follow all the laws. I think I would like to be a police officer.)

Day 5

All answers will vary.

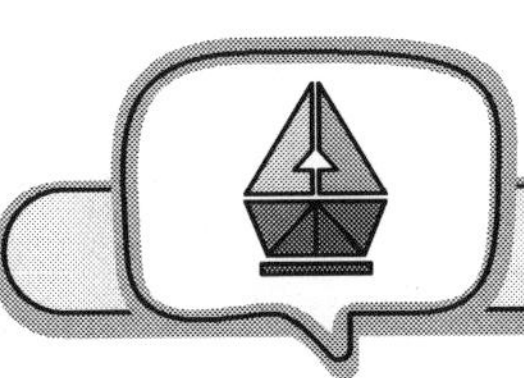

Week 7

Day 1

1. C
2. B
3. D
4. A and B

Day 2

1. Yes
2. Yes
3. No
4. No
5. Yes

Day 3

Answers will vary. (Examples will be similar to the descriptions given in the activity from Day 2)

Day 4

Answers will vary. (Example: I think being the President would be a hard job because they are in charge of so many people. I would not like to be the President because I would not want people to be mad at me.)

Day 5

Answers will vary. (Example: If I were President of the United States, I would make sure everybody had enough food to eat.)

Week 8

Day 1

1. False
2. True
3. C
4. A, B and C

Day 2

1. Yes
2. No
3. Yes
4. Yes
5. No

Day 3

Answers will vary. (Example: The American flag is important to me because my uncle is in the military and fought for our freedom.)

Answers will vary. (Example: school, police station, a neighbor's house)

Day 4

Answers will vary.

Day 5

Answers will vary. (Example: The White House is another important American symbol because it is where our President lives.)

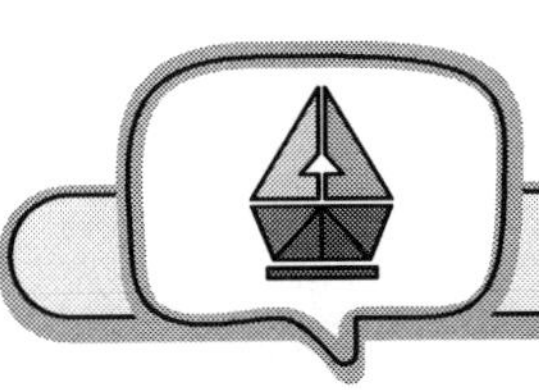

Week 9

Day 1

1. False
2. True
3. B
4. True

Day 2

Answers will vary. (Examples might include: Clean up my toys before bedtime. Listen when others are speaking.)

Day 3

Answers will vary. (Examples might include: It is important to listen when others are speaking because we can learn from what others have to say.)

Day 4

Answers will vary.

Day 5

Answers will vary. (Example: Rules are important because they keep us safe.)

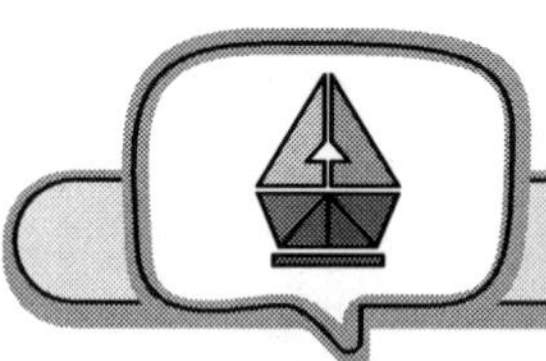

Week 10

Day 1

1. B
2. False
3. True
4. True

Day 2

Answers will vary. (Examples might include: Sunnyside Heights, Springfield, Missouri, United States, North America)

Day 3

Answers will vary. (Examples might include: Follow the laws or rules. Be kind to others. Take care of shared spaces.)

Day 4

1. Answers will vary. (Example: It is important to me to be a good citizen because it means I am helping take care of my community.)
2. Answers will vary. (Example: I am a good citizen at school by always listening to my teacher.)
3. Answers will vary. (Example: I am a good citizen of my city/state by picking up trash at the playground.)

Day 5

Answers will vary.

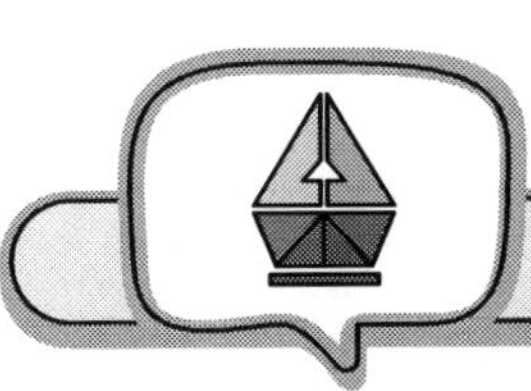

Week 11

Day 1

1. True
2. A
3. B
4. C

Day 2

1. Continent - 2
2. Ocean - 4
3. River - 1
4. Highway - 5
5. Forest - 3

Day 3

Answers will vary. (See below for examples)

Same: Map and globes show many of the same features. Maps and globes help us locate places in the world.

Different: Maps are flat drawings and globes are round. Maps can show just a small part of the world and globes show the entire world.

Day 4

All answers will vary.

Day 5

Answers will vary. (Examples might include: I created a map of my school. The special features I included are: the gym, the cafeteria, the playground, and my classroom. I know I created a map, not a globe, because my drawing is flat.)

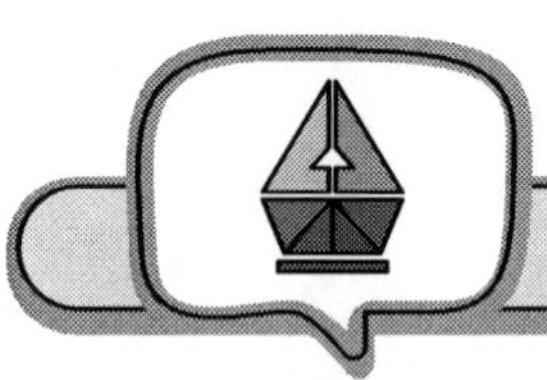

Week 12

Day 1

1. D
2. False
3. True
4. B

Day 2

All answers will vary.

Day 3

Answers will vary. (See below for example)

My address is 123 Elm Street, Indianapolis, Indiana 46201. It is important that I know my address because I may need to give it to someone if there is an emergency. It is ok to give my address to the following people: family members, a police officer, a firefighter, or my teacher.

Day 4

All answers will vary.

Day 5

Answers will vary. (Examples might include: Mom, Dad, Grandma, Aunt Sue, my neighbor Bill)

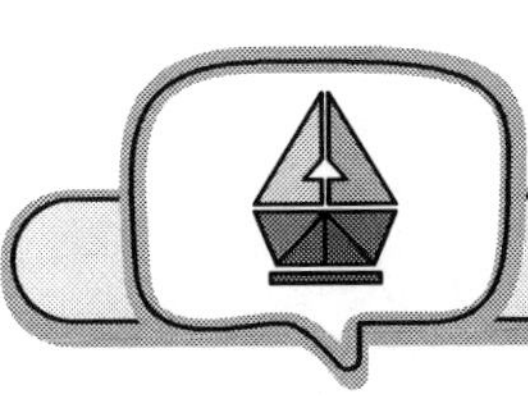

Week 13

Day 1

1. True
2. B
3. True
4. C

Day 2

Table: Answers will vary. (Examples might include: Winter - cold and snowy, Spring - cool and rainy, Summer - sunny and hot, Fall - cool and windy with some sun)

Day 3

All answers will vary. (Examples might include: In winter, I like to build snowmen and snow forts. In summer, I like to go swimming at the pool.)

Day 4

Table: Answers will vary. (Examples might include: Winter - heavy coats, mittens, scarves and a hat, Spring - raincoat and rain boots, Summer - shorts and a tank top, Fall - light jacket and pants)

Day 5

All answers will vary. (Examples might include: In winter, I wear snow pants, boots, gloves, and a hat to play outside in the snow. In summer, I wear a swimsuit to swim in the pool.)

Week 14

Day 1

1. True
2. C
3. False
4. D

Day 2

1. Clothing, music, food, language, art, holidays/celebrations
2. Interview someone from a different culture, research a different culture in books or on the internet

Day 3

All answers will vary. (Examples might include: tools, customs, beliefs, type of houses)

Day 4

Answers will vary. (See below for examples)

Similarities: language, food

Differences: clothing, type of house, celebrations, art

Day 5

All answers will vary. (Examples might include: Drawing pictures of the different houses each group lives in or the clothing they wear.)

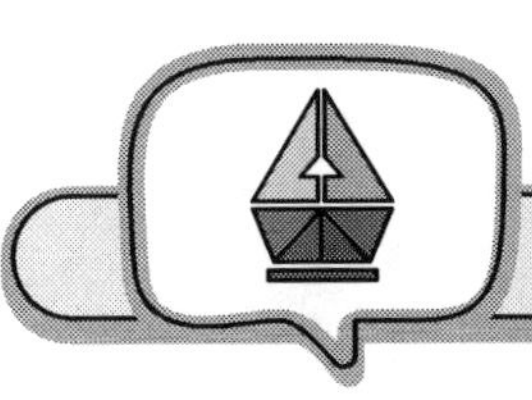

Week 15

Day 1

1. D
2. True
3. False
4. B and D

Day 2

Answers will vary. (Examples might include: using single-use straws and water bottles or killing bees)

Day 3

All answers will vary. (Examples might include: Using plastic straws is harmful to the environment because they end up in the landfill.)

Day 4

Answers will vary. (Examples might include: buying resuable straws, bags, and water bottles or cleaning up trash on the street)

Day 5

All answers will vary. (Examples might include: To improve the environment, I picked up litter on the school playground. This is helpful because it makes the playground look nicer, and animals won't eat the trash on the ground.)

Week 16

Day 1

1. B
2. False
3. True
4. A

Day 2

Answers will vary. (See examples below)

Wants: a video game, a tablet, a basketball hoop, a bike

Needs: food, a house, clothes, shoes

Day 3

All answers will vary. (Examples might include: I want a computer. I know this is a want because I don't have to have it to live. It would just make life more fun.)

Day 4

Answers will vary. (See examples below)

Wants: museum visits, restaurant visits

Needs: an apartment, furniture, work clothes, taxi fare

Day 5

All answers will vary. (Examples might include: The first thing I think Suzi should buy is an apartment. I think this because she needs a place to live. I don't think Suzi should spend any money on eating at restaurants because she has a lot of needs that should be taken care of first.)

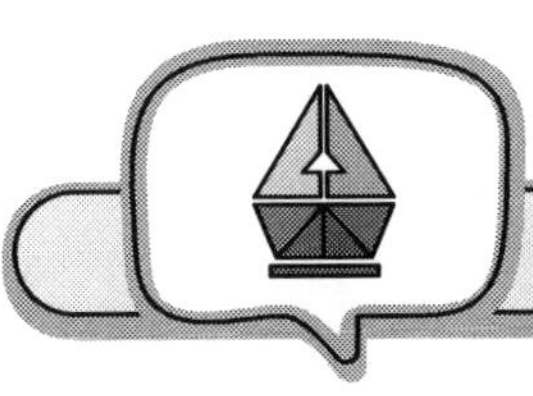

Week 17

Day 1

1. C
2. True
3. False
4. D

Day 2

Answers will vary. (Examples might include: veterinarian, waitress, baseball player, banker)

Day 3

All answers will vary. (Examples might include: A veterinarian's job is to take care of animals and make sure they stay healthy.)

Day 4

1. Preschool teacher/kindergarten teacher/daycare worker
2. Waitress/server
3. Construction worker
4. Delivery driver
5. Baker

Day 5

All answers will vary.

Week 18

Day 1

1. A, B, D
2. False
3. True
4. True

Day 2

Answers will vary. (Examples might include: Hairdresser - styling tools, hair dye, scissors)

Day 3

All answers will vary. (Examples might include: A veterinarian uses a stethoscope to make sure animals are healthy.)

Day 4

1. D
2. A
3. C
4. B

Day 5

All answers will vary.

Week 19

Day 1

1. A, C
2. True
3. False
4. B

Day 2

1. B
2. C
3. D
4. A

Day 3

All answers will vary. (Examples might include: People choose certain jobs because they like something or are good at something.)

Day 4

All answers will vary.

Day 5

All answers will vary.

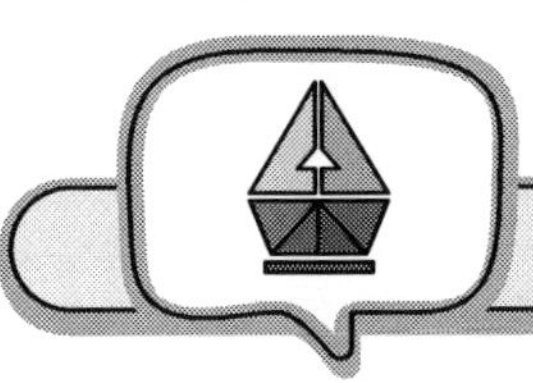

Answer Key

Week 20

Day 1

1. D
2. True
3. False
4. True

Day 2

Yes	No
Cleaning the bathroom	Seeing patients
Making phone calls	Caring for zoo animals
Teaching children	Stocking grocery store shelves
Doing homework	Driving a bus

Day 3

All answers will vary. (Examples might include: People can teach children from home. I know this because my mom homeschools my brother and me.)

Day 4

All answers will vary (Examples might include: mopping floors, taking out the trash, doing homework, cleaning my bedroom, making my bed)

Day 5

All answers will vary. (Examples might include: I do work at home by making my bed every morning before school.)

KIDS WINTER ACADEMY

Kids Winter Academy by ArgoPrep covers material learned in September through December so your child can reinforce the concepts they should have learned in class. We recommend using this particular series during the winter break. This workbook includes two weeks of activities for math, reading, science, and social studies. Best of all, you can access detailed video explanations to all the questions on our website.

Made in the USA
Las Vegas, NV
29 April 2024